MANOSOPHY

MANOSOPHY

A GAMEPLAN FOR YOUR LIFE

Stephen "Pops" Cohen

MANOSOPHY
A GAMEPLAN FOR YOUR LIFE

iUniverse books may be ordered through booksellers or by contacting:

iUniverse
1663 Liberty Drive
Bloomington, IN 47403
www.iuniverse.com
1-800-Authors (1-800-288-4677)

ISBN: 978-1-5320-3962-1 (sc)
ISBN: 978-1-5320-3963-8 (e)

Print information available on the last page.

iUniverse rev. date: 12/21/2017

*For Josh, Gabe, Andrew, and Stephanie and the
next generation of men, Harrison and West*

CONTENTS

PROLOGUE

"All men are created equal endowed by
their creator with certain UNALIENABLE
rights, and that among these are LIFE,
LIBERTY, and, THE PURSUIT of
HAPPINESS"

Declaration of Independence July 1776

The Power of Transformation

As a man in a free society you have the right to happiness. It is not a privilege, nor is it granted by a government to you.

The framers of the Constitution believed, free men had these rights and they could not be surrendered, sold, or transferred by those in power. The pursuit of a man's destiny was to be of his own design, not at the behest of a monarch. These "natural rights" were part of a social contract that men struck between these inherent freedoms and the government that existed to protect them from forces that would restrict them.

Finding happiness is not nearly as easily obtained as stated. Most men ramble through life taking on significant responsibilities, of family and home, wind up in some series of jobs, roles and pursuits. Usually, it is without a plan, regular consideration, or introspection. The result is a society of men who are dissatisfied with their own development, sense of self worth, and their future. Often the pursuit of happiness, is about someone else's desires and needs, and yours are left in second place.

It is the purpose of this book to provide a handbook for you to develop your own philosophy of life that is unique to the modern man, a Manosophy. It will offer a design to create your "personal operating system" that will offer you a distinct game plan to direct your life along a path you can pursue with enthusiasm and conviction. Even if you decide to take no action, reject the outlook of a game plan, and decide to just live your life as you are now, the exercises and pure thinking about your life, will bring you some more peace of mind.

Manosophy has a simple premise. You can become the best person you can be. Where you are now, in mind, body, and spirit can be better, transformed. You have a greatness inside yourself that can be revealed and become exhibited, or manifest. This will not happen by only thinking it or dreaming it. Transformation requires a game plan, direction and finally, action in the direction of your goal. The power of a philosophy comes from taking steps to achieve the results you desire.

And, there is no reason to be put off by the idea of having a philosophy of how to live your life. Philosophy is a manly pursuit that raises some fundamental questions, worth pondering.

What do I believe

What is my purpose

What are my guiding principles

How do I achieve my purpose

What is Right and Wrong (Ethics)

What is my Game Plan to Achieve Happiness

Men of all types and from all disciplines have offered their view of what makes for a complete life philosophy. They range from belief in a life predetermined by God or a celestial force, where you have little "free will" in your life; to, the hedonists,who believe life is about finding and pursuing pleasure for it's own sake. Along, the way we will explore many theoretical constructs, and the best philosophy for your life will reveal itself.

For perspective, we need only to reflect upon the life long study of Joseph Campbell, who in *The Hero with a Thousand Faces*, examined the world's religion's and the underlying mythology of faith. In this study, he discovered that successful societies expected men to "follow your bliss". He found that as men pursued what filled them up, society found it's way to achievement, progress and a meaningful balance of forces. Now that is not to say that this pursuit of bliss was a simple, smooth path. The man, in the case of founding mythology, was often the hero of the story, who fought powerful forces externally, but more so, internally to get to his goal. The heroes journey was the essential archetype of the societies he studied, and he, concluded, that we all have our own heroic quest for happiness, and we must battle like warriors to complete our own journeys.

You know about the journey of the hero. You are living it. Campbell's men were sent on these paths by the Gods, or the Forces. You may not think you are Odysseus, Luke Skywalker, or even, Rocky Balboa but you are on a path of similar challenges. Your life has it's own story arc that includes finding a way to make a living, dealing with family, spouses, girlfriends, children, finances, and your general well being. All of these challenges can become energizing and fulfilling episodes or obstacles to your own fulfillment and pursuit of your goals.

Transformation emerges from a philosophy. The philosophy, however, needs to be yours, not that of your family, parents or the woman in your life. Manosophy is about listening to your yearnings to become what you want to become. A personal operating system is based upon the following premise:

We are all capable of transformation. One incremental step towards a goal, like wellness or a new career direction, or a new manner of speech and carriage. Just one full glass of water a day, a cupcake uneaten, a smile when you are low, are steps towards a better you. You can decide to be fuller, brighter, lighter, and more at peace with your life, or decide to scream at the forces. It is your choice. But transformation requires one step up the Everest of your life, just one, affirmation that you can progress along a new path. It is about being present as you choose the next thing, one moment linked to another, one step over another, upward. It is about aspirations, inspiring yourself, and moving towards the best of yourself.

It requires resolve to develop a philosophy for yourself. It also means allowing yourself the time and pure joy of examining the life you want, as a process. It is as important as your work, your family, and your health. But, men have an Olympian capacity to avoid these questions, and often choose instead to remain where they are, and let life just happen, based upon an operating system that is not theirs. The usual excuse is "work".

Some of the great, modern philosophers were working men. They did not have the luxury of sitting in academia or the porches of ancient Greece and contemplate the working of the world. Eric Hoffer, was a longshoreman, who survived alcoholism and jail wrote in the *True Believer*, how the failure of poor self esteem, made men more susceptible to mass movements and authoritarianism. He wrote a syndicated news column on how life works, all the while going to work at the docks. His calloused hands and rough life brought a workingman's sensibility to living a simple but honest life .

Charles Bukowski was a poet, who wrote about his life "fighting the forces" of booze, women, and gambling on ponies, and a life lived large. From his small apartments, he hacked out prose that created a philosophy of life from his world view. He wrote on paper bags, between jobs. He sorted mail to support his life and his habits. In his many volumes of poetry and novels, his recurrent theme was that a man could fight the "forces" with stamina, humor, and not attaching himself to outcomes imposed by society.

This book offers you that same opportunity to think about your life, and it's direction. It is for you to decide what you want to change, keep the same, or redirect. At the end of each chapter, we'll ask WHAT ARE YOU PREPARED TO DO?

You can decide to take no action on the proposed tasks. You can delay them. You can also plot some activity that will begin the incremental steps to transform your sense of who you want to become and your new path.

Electing to create a Manosophy for your life, and a personal operating system, will transform you. The unalienable rights you have will be honored, and you and those around you will become better people and citizens. No one can win a game, let alone live a life, without a game plan that has heart and is based upon the best of our abilities. This does not mean that just having a plan guarantees a winning and fulfilled life, anymore than a great game plan in sports guarantees victory. But, we do know that without a plan, we are at the mercy of the plan of someone else, no matter, how well meaning, it is their plan for us, not our own.

This is an opportunity to create your game plan, your Manosophy. A chance to understand what you believe and the life you want to pursue. It will take courage to think about it, create, it and do it.

But you can do this. You have the right to pursue your happiness. You have the right to own your life.

WHAT ARE YOU PREPARED TO DO
Respond to Questions to Create Profile

State of Mind

- Are you learning what you need

- Do you usually find yourself engaged in fulfilling or enjoyable thinking
- Are you growing or expanding your knowledge
- Do you find you can focus on tasks
- Is your mind at peace most days
- Does anger or frustration enter into your day with frequency

Body

- Do you fell strong
- Are you within a good weight to height ratio
- Do you consume what you like and need
- Is physical activity a routine in your life
- Are you fighting addictions
- Do you put your fitness as a high priority

Spirit

- Do you feel at peace most days
- Is love part of your life
- Are your relationships life enhancing
- Do you take time to use techniques to release stress and anxiety
- Are you connected to some higher source, God, or faith, does it matter to you

Now weigh your responses to offer yourself an initial profile of what is working or not in life, as it is now. You will know quickly, if it is going well, or needs improvement in certain areas.

CHAPTER I

Beer, Broads, Balls

"God is Great, Beer is Good, People are Crazy"

Billy Currington 2009
People are Crazy

A young man bumps into an older fellow at a bar somewhere in Ohio. Over a few beers, and a country tune, they exchange their views on life. It is a good time, as they review woman, divorce, the role of God in their lives, and outlook on themselves and the world around them. It is the context of a popular country song, that suggests the unique observation of the writer and philosopher, Billy Currington.

It is these observations of life when seen from afar, in this case, in the words of a man at the end of his life, that offer some insight into how a person views the meaning of life, or how life seems to work. These observations do not make up a philosophy of life, but, offers indicators of how a person might have approached the day to day reality of

1

their journey. For Currington's fictional old man, you could imagine he enjoyed his beer, had some faith in a higher power, and had a whimsical, lighter view of the character of those that passed through his life.

Many of these observations on life become slogans for living. They offer some insight on directions we might take, but do not constitute a game plan, or course of action. And often, these observations can be powerful negative forces that hold men back from establishing a view of themselves and their world that leads to happiness.

The development of a Manosophy is subversive. It challenges current stereotypes of what motivates modern men. To be sure men have interests and lifestyles that go beyond drinking beer with his buddies; an obsession with beautiful women; and a constant attention to watching and playing sports. There is,of course, not a damn thing wrong with these pursuits; but, as a prime definition of men, it is abhorrent. It is an observation adopted my mass media, enhanced by a pro- feminist battleground theory, of them or us mentality, and adopted by millions of women as the accepted view of men in their world.

Manosophy is not about achieving happiness at the expense of women, or not respecting their efforts to find their own operating systems. It is not a zero sum game. If we achieve what we desire, it does not mean the women in your life cannot be a partner and participant in your journey. In fact, men and women on the same path to self –realization offers a significant advantage to success. This is the logic of Manosophy, but not necessarily the approach of women in media and power. Men are often positioned as at fault for problems, barriers to enlightenment, and, by extension, the reason for the obstacles that confront women.

A philosophy that demeans women, or posits them as the source and barrier to your peace of mind is hollow. It gives them a power to contain you that is precisely why developing an operating system is critical to your well being. Societies that seek to limit women's rights, restrict educational opportunity, and force inequality have not elevated the station of men. They have only offered a restriction of liberty and dampened economic and political stability. Misogyny is a flawed outlook that does not elevate men, but diminishes them. You can have a philosophy that celebrates women who accept you and your quest for self fulfillment. You can embrace women who honor your approach to life, and leave those who do not out of your world view.

When Germaine Greer wrote the *Female Eunuch* in 1970, she posited the role of men, as hating women, and that led to women hating themselves. Her distain was so great that she wrote of a battle between women in search of joy, and men who were responsible for cutting women off from their libido and natural desires. She would have them all symbolically emasculated. Betty Freidan, served a more moderate, but more influential role with a more balanced view. In her 1963, *Feminine Mystique*, women were seen as in search of a broader life than provided by being a "housewife". She called it "A Problem that had No Name." She called for women to rally around certain precepts that sustained a more evolved woman, including equal pay for same jobs, and equality in relationships. These feminist ideals spawned affirmative action, sexual harassment guidelines, maternal leave, family medical leave, more equality in the workplace, higher pay, and a sexual revolution, where women expected to be equal partners in the bedroom.

These feminist concerns also changed equality in schools, and woman's sports with Title IX sanctions that asked for, and got, equal treatment for woman's sports, in terms of facilities and range of activities. Feminism also targeted woman's health issues and research dollars for work in a wide range of diseases from ovarian and breast cancer, to the creation of a movement to protect woman's rights for abortion.

Later day benefactors of these efforts included a proliferation of women pundits and pop psychologists, who through mass media managed to offer an inspirational message to women. The high priestess of the theory of abundance, self analysis, and an examined, but joy filled life was, of course, talk show host and iconic heroine, Oprah Winfrey. The Oprah Nation exerted an enormous influence offering a moderate view of the feminist ideals, while offering women encouragement to review their lives. Oprah offered evolution for a modern woman towards happiness that was not centered in the "smug and arrogant" viewpoints of the movements founders.

It was out of her personal experiences and sense of what values were needed to create a better life for her audience, that she offered a message with it's own language, attitude and results. It was her genius to transfer her sense of "knowing" who needed tools and encouragement to find the best path for themselves. This was accomplished in her later years, without rancor,or a need to demonize men. Although, by her own admission, in the beginning years men were often targeted as the main obstacle to a woman's spiritual renewal.

As feminism flowered, the image of men and what they were about floundered.

Men were encouraged to be open about their feelings, share household duties, listen more, adapt to the needs and concerns of the emerging feminine mystique. The partnership promised a stronger relationship, a second household income, and an opportunity to be released from some of the pressures of shouldering the responsibilities of being the primary wage earner and provider.

Some of this happened, but, for most men, married and not, they became more detached from the core questions of their lives. Who am I? What is my purpose? What is my passion? How do I achieve a degree of happiness?

For some, they became distant from families, were not present actually or figuratively, and searched in some form of silent desperation to unlock the mystery of their lives. All men are part of that brotherhood, faced by an onslaught of restrictive and negative imagery, we often found solace in retreat from our futures, rather than an enthusiastic embrace of the next thing.

The trap is believing the slogans that men are defined by beer, broads, and balls. Having an effective operating system based upon a Manosophy you develop, requires a view of life without limits. Understanding some basic approaches to life and their meaning can help start the process of discovery and offer insights into your philosophical tenets.

SOME SLOGANS

"It's Out of Your Hands'

Predestination versus Free Will

You might be surprised to find many of your friends who believe that life is already charted for you. This approach believes that, at least, in broad strokes, what happens to you is "meant to be". This supposes that the predestination of your life is in the hands of some larger force, a God, or for less religious types, just the way the world works for people like them.

This outlook is at it's most powerful at the end of a life. When someone remarks, it was their time to go, with that fatal accident. Or, the" bullet had his name on it". In the movie, the *Last Samurai*, Ken Watanabe, as Katsumoto remarks to the Tom Cruise character, Nathan Algren, at the end of a battle, ' It was not your time". Such poignancy suggests an invisible hand over the end game, but, it does not mean that a well lived life is simply a matter that is predetermined.

Even if one believes the end of existence, or the passage from this life to another state, is known to the universe, it does not negate the choices made day to day.

Philosophers who are stepped in faith based theology have often pondered the existence of free will in such theoretical constructs. Can you have free will in a predetermined life? And does it mean that your choices are also selected to lead you to the only path you could take?

As fanciful as these arguments may seem, the reality is that is obvious from observation that many men choose to live their lives as though they have no free will, and are destined to the life they are given by design or circumstance.

Free will suggests that you can make choices. Each choice has it's consequence that may be apparent at that moment or not seen for years to follow. People who believe in free will, believe options are always available, and can change the course of a man's destiny.

The challenge in the world of free will is to make good choices, that have value. Choices that Don Juan Matus, Carlos Castaneda's sorcerer guide in *The Teachings of Don Juan*, would call a "good path". To don Juan, "Look at every path closely, then ask yourself this question.. Does this path have a heart? If it does, then the path is good. If it doesn't it is of no use." Castaneda found the process of finding a path with heart, hardly a simple process, it required great self reflection, some peyote, and finally a deep sense of knowing.

"Shit Happens"

Stoicism

This is the current short form definition of what classicists call Stoicism. Stoics believed that things happen in life that are unexplained, some that come from direct causes, and other that are just part of living a life as free man. Obviously what does happen can be totally random, or the result of some series of events or circumstances. To the Stoic it does not matter the causation, as much as the response. Stoics respond to most events in proportion to their impact on your life. If a stone bounces off the road and cracks your windshield, you can take it as a sign of driving too close to the truck in front of you; you can scream and moan and attempt to catch the truck driver, or, you can acknowledge it happened, get it fixed and go on. A stoic takes the last choice.

Life goes on, things happen. How you respond makes you wise or a fool.

The Stoics of the Third Century B.C believed as did Epictetus that the "subject of the art of living is your life"

Knowledge was revealed by reason, and the reaction to events revealed your nature. These stoics offered a popular outlook that fit their times, since they functioned in a highly structured class society. It allowed the ruling class, including emperor, Marcus Aurelius to offer an understanding to all classes that life could be difficult, but all events could be handled in a stoic's view.

From their "painted porches", where stoicism derives it's name, stoics talked through the way their lives were impacted by events. It made sense to the ancients to take most of it as it came to them. The dilemma, of course, comes if what happens is unjust, damages freedom, or subverts the human spirit. The Stoic answer may not be good enough for such circumstances.

Sometimes when "s…t happens ", things must change. Taking things as they come may not be enough in an operating system that has justice and right in it's philosophy.

"Live Like You Are Dying"

Life is Short

The overall theme here is of urgency, and, a sense of not knowing when life is over.

This slogan requires some sense of what is valued in the personal operating system, since the very acceleration of what might be left undone demands a notion of what it is you want. If you desire a trip to Paris; to learn how to play bass guitar; look up your high school sweetheart; all require some choice that these things were important enough to get scheduled into your plan, and quickly.

To artist,Tim McGraw, in his song of the same slogan;

he went skydiving, Rocky Mountain Climbing, road a bull named Fu Manchu, and became sweeter, loved deeper, and "offered forgiveness I've been denying."

It's a worthwhile exercise to write down what you would for a week if you were writing McGraw's lyrics for your song? Would you be agreeable to more people, tell your gal you love her, visit with your parents, write a poem? Or would you be more global and serious; write your Congressman, tell your boss what you really think; play all night Texas Hold' Em or just do what makes you feel good?

You might find it's a pretty long list of approaches to people, ideas and life. Then you need to figure out how you get it all accomplished, if the end was coming. How would you prioritize what you want to do?

Ask yourself the question; What would I do now, If I knew I was dying?

Approach this exercise on the basis of your current resources, don't hype it up, as though, you just hit the Lotto. Take a serious inventory of the questions, write down your thoughts and hold onto them.

"Everything will turn out for the Best"

Optimism

A slogan that suggests a positive outlook that empowers believers to enjoy the present moment and to expect that the next will be as worthwhile. It is also used as defense mechanism to assist a person in hard times, to encourage forbearance. Not unlike predestination it is a slogan that fits a person who finds himself in difficult circumstances. If you were a serf in feudal Europe, while you might not ever see you situation and class status changing could expect a better day, or at least, look at your lot from it's own narrow circumstance; while you are a serf you can live within your class and still be optimistic about your future. Optimism also fuels a belief that a life can evolve to better circumstances.

This cultivation of outlook is an aspect of a life that you can control whether living within a free society or under a repressive regime. You can select your outlook, regardless of circumstance, and force a belief system in a new reality or outcome. Victor Frankl lived part of his life in Auschwitz concentration camp. He knew his wife and parents were murdered, and he saw his companions take sick, and others die before him. In his seminal book on these experiences, *Man's Search for Meaning*, he offered the theory that people who had a positive, and optimistic outlook seemed better able to deal with the horror of imprisonment in the camp. This did not mean their lot was any better, actually, they were as likely to die at the hands of the Nazi's as the next person. But, optimism made them "hardy" and able to handle the present moment, while holding onto hope that the next moment would be, if not, better, sustainable. Their hope could be based upon faith, a vision of angels, or the belief that all life had some meaning, but, all overcame the "emptiness of life" and existential despair by a belief in a better moment.

Of course, like the other slogans we have reviewed, optimism has its limits. It can force a false sense of well being. Seeing the world as an optimist can cloud the obvious reality, and you can misread your options and need to action in life, if you are not analytical of your positive outlook. Optimism can shield reality, and keep you from taking steps to improve your life, because you think it will get better by wishing it to be so. French writer, Enlightenment philosopher of the 18th century, Voltaire expressed the dangers in his classic, satiric tale of the young man, *Candide.* It is the story of a man who finds his life journey, from relationships to politics, is better when he takes a positive outlook. However, his friend and mentor Pangloss is the eternal optimist and says, "all is for the best, in the best of all possible worlds," and moves through the story unable to see the decline of freedom and repression that surrounds himself, the country and his friend Candide. Pangloss' optimism eventually lands him in poor circumstances, in jail and eventually hung for his failure to see the truth of things, which he avoided in this tale at all costs. Voltaire gets his point across, that Panglossian optimism is as dangerous as unwarranted pessimism.

Still, choosing an outlook that is based upon this slogan can offer the sense that your path will have some clear, unhindered patches.

"It's Karma Man"

Karmic Debt

The concept of karma has a certain complexity to it that goes beyond cause and effect. At it's root karma was part of an operating system, or way of life that flowed from an understanding of the precepts of Buddha. In this belief system there are ways to overcome human suffering, through right action, and right thinking. This eight fold path, as described by Lama Surya Das in, *Awakening the Buddha Within*, requires a devotion to the simple act of all faith based systems, "doing the right thing'. The penalty for wrong thinking and action can be described as a debt you owe the universe, and those around for a error in judgment or wrong headed action.

Karma is often seen in a simple context of cause and effect. If you do something harmful or someone else does, it returns, at some point in bad karma. To Buddhists, of course, this accumulation of karmic debt may not be repaid until many lives later, or on the karmic wheel of the next life, your debt is repaid, and you spend the next life in greater suffering, or devoting a life to penance.

There is no doubt, however, that we can all feel a vibration from people who do good works in our lives, and those who are out for themselves. Sometimes you may find a person who truly embodies evil, and you feel uncomfortable in their presence, or seek to respond to triumph over them with your own nobility. Bad vibes, as they are called, are real and palpable. We all have vibrations of energy, and we can through work on our lives, assert better feelings, project positive energy, and be more likely to achieve our goals when aware of cause and effect.

Still relying on "karma" as a way of creating a unified philosophy has it's flaws. While you can control your energy, utterances and actions, you can't know how the actions of others will impact you. The karma that surrounds you is part of a vast series of causations that may or may not propel you forward.

Awareness of the impact of your actions can propel good results, and right thinking, to use the Buddhist term, can resonate with any philosophy for your life.

WHAT ARE YOU PREPARED TO DO

As always we suggest, you can do these exercises now. You can continue reading and come back to them. Or, you can acknowledge them and do the work when you want or not at all.

WHAT SLOGAN DO YOU HAVE FOR YOUR LIFE?

CREATE A SLOGAN THAT OFFERS YOU DIRECTION

IF YOU ARE ASKED WHAT YOU WANT IN LIFE, WHAT WOULD YOU SAY ?

WHO or WHAT IS THE GREATEST INFLUENCE ON YOUR LIFE GOALS?

CHAPTER II

Create Your Pop Personal Operating Philosophy

It is not what you want you attract ... you
attract what you believe to be true

Neville Goddard

We all go through each day with some internal system. It sets the trajectory for the day ahead. Our actions fall into patterns, our motions, utterances and actions are more often than not unexamined. Yet, it all happens because we have developed a view of our lives based upon a way of life, or operating pattern. This pattern is actually a philosophy, a view of our world based upon our take on who we are, what we want, and how we see everything.

A personal operating philosophy is a conscious plan of action that makes you wake up to what life you want for yourself. It is based upon core beliefs, and an analysis of the people and circumstances that are unique to you. It requires no advanced courses or seminars to create, only your realization that the life you are living may not be the life you want. This gap between what is and what you want is the essential reality of philosophic thought.

All a philosophy does is give you a roadmap, a game plan to follow to actually close the gap between where you are and what you feel, and a life that fulfills your innermost yearnings. You have to develop this POP to figure out how to get it, achieve it over time, and not destroy everything you have in the process.

For the sake of understanding philosophical precepts, some start with Pythagoras around 500 BCE. His ancient Greek yearnings led him to attempt to discern the simple ideal way to live, what was just and just, what was real. And through it all was anything, he did determined by free will or destiny and an array of Gods or superstitions.

And through the ages, philosophical thought continued to deal with these same concerns, each defined by the age when these questions were asked. Socrates begat Plato who taught Aristotle. Greeks yielded to Romans like Seneca. There were Stoics, Cynics, and Hedonists. Pursuit of pure pleasure; the avoidance of conflict and pain; fealty to the divine as pagans, the divine as Christ, and just God's will.

Eventually more humanist philosophies evolved that extolled helping others, the old Golden Rule, and a sense that we were the masters of our universe and the guardian of our souls, regardless of the nut cases that surrounded us. This included the favorite of Nietzsche, the will to power; Buddha's you will suffer, but you can temper it by following the right paths; and the purpose of life is to be happy or follow your bliss. Even, professor Timothy Leary weighed in with a world view for his times ; to turn on, tune in, and drop out, and just enjoy the hell out of the trip you are on.

Putting aside the acid trip, we have evolved to popular culture amalgams of any of the above,so called, "schools" of thought. Neo in the Matrix wonders what is real. He takes a red pill to find out. Luke Skywalker challenges a world where evil is obvious and in control and the Jedi fight to restore an order based on their philosophy of the power of good within; and winning NFL teams have coaches that preach discipline, study, fitness, and the overwhelming power of the community effort, the team.

There continues this search for mastery of your life. What are the keys. And once found how do you chalkboard the plays that will bring you to a sense of peace and power about who you are, want to be, and where it will all take you.

It begins with how do you see the world and your place within it?

This is where Manosophy starts and how a personal operating philosophy is created. It is not fancy, difficult or obtuse. We are after a POP that is useable, direct, and actionable.

OUTLOOK

Do you see the life you live in a positive, uplifting light? Do you perceive much of what you do with a certain darkness? Of course, you may have moments where you insert different feelings about circumstances or events. Still, if you charted your days, and labeled them, would you find a basically bright place on this chart of your life?

Given the exact same circumstances and events, different

men have different views of their circumstances. The details may be identical, but different results are extracted. This is because one guys outlook on any task can be quite different than an others.

Jake and Aaron have the same requirements at lacrosse practice. They run in pads for a mile and do repetitive passing drills before practice games. They both dislike the task, but Jake approaches it with vigor and drops his oppositions once he is on the field. Aaron does not, he complains and rarely gets the same work out as Jake. Aaron has superior,inherent talents, but is fatigued, angry and resentful most days. Jake with less skills, still enjoys his after school practices, and plays well in games.

Here talent is not an issue, but outlook defines each player. You can have superior skills and still enjoy the mundane tasks, if a more upbeat and hardy outlook guides you. The problem with a negative outlook, is not about success, it is about creating a positive, hary, internal environment that gives you enormous power to realize your potential It is just more difficult to achieve, and manifest your talents when you exhibit and possess a sour outlook.

Obviously, there is a balance to this aspect of our belief system. Optimism at all times may be unrealistic, as is eternal pessimism. Yet, even in the worst circumstances a bright outlook seems to offer more for survival and success of,even the most dire condition. Again, noted philosopher and psychiatrist, Viktor Frankl found the most successful prisoners at the Nazi death camps, lived longer, and were better able to cope with their plight who had some outlook that was not seeped in their obvious precarious present state. Similarly, stories of pilots incarcerated in the infamous, Hanoi Hilton, Senator John McCain found that maintaining an outlook where they controlled their view of their circumstances sustained them through years of torture and malnourishment.

Even, the brave souls on the Bataan death march, including those who eventually succumbed to severe depravations, did better if they had hope, controlled there thinking, and did not allow their captors to dictate their world view.

Outlook Inventory

Over the next four weeks, be aware of your outlook. Do you find at the end of each day, that it was more a negative, or did you get a feeling of accomplishment or just the satisfaction of getting through another day.

Most of our days, as modern men, are packed with events and competing claims on our attention, energy and can pull us away from our goals. It takes enormous focus to begin to carve out enough of any given day, to dedicate towards the life we want to achieve and that we hope will, eventually, become our lives. Yet, the less we devote to carving out time, even if delayed, to a weekend or time off, the more likely we are to be off point, and living someone else's POP, and not our own.

Your outlook is not about tasks and what you get done. It is about what you think about any of them. The more you approach these tasks as a part of your learning, a way to show and grow skills, the more powerful you become. Even the most mundane, hated task, can be done and passed along, without catching too much of you.

It sums up easily- but requires being awake and aware to accomplish it:

There is NOTHING I cannot handle. The things I must do, I WILL DO .

Whatever I do will be MADE BETTER. The things I HAVE to DO that I do not like, WILL NOT DRAIN ME of my energy or attack my soul.

I will live each day in ACCORDANCE WITH MY PHILOSOPHY, and allow me to achieve the life I WANT FOR MYSELF.

WINS AND LOSSES- THE WORLD IS ONE BIG COMPETITION

This one of the most common working philosophies for modern men. There is a sense, instilled, from childhood that our entire existence is a playing field where there is always a winner and a loser. It is essentially a view of competition and engenders behaviors that achieve success, either within a moral code or, even, outside of it if a W can be achieved.

It posits what happens in life as following certain rules of the game. Someone serves to judge the game and actions, and against those rules, and odds (the forces), life plays out. As an analogy for life, it serve as valid philosophical premise. Because so much of what we confront in life appears as a competition.

The Competition as Life Force

Often, we confront conflict between forces as the manner our life seems to move forward and progress:

Education: will our SATs and LSATs get us into the best schools. Will our grades excel, can I achieve in contest with others for scholarships, monetary loans, the best training

Jobs: will our background and achievements get the job I require. Or, will another achieve the role I desire.

Love and Marriage: will I find the right person, fall in love, sustain a successful marriage; and raise children; who are my rivals in this quest

Wealth and Security: can I compete with others who are on track for the same goals, am I the hammer or the nail,in this critical area of life.

All of the above are legitimate concerns, you can chart a W or an L. But who are you really fighting against in this battle? It may seem, and is, in the short range the adversary. They are real, to be sure. But, the POP requires that you wrestle within yourself on these matters. The real opponent is what is going on inside of your psyche.

In fact, your very ability to win, is contained in your view of how you will perform against the onslaught of external challengers. It is not that competition does not exist, but, that the way to achieving what you desire comes from a mindset that opens the way to success.

WINNING IS AN INTERNAL ACT

All competition and success starts inside each man's belief system. It begins with a thought of what can be achieved, what is desired, and how to achieve it. Acting as though, you are already the successful individual, whether athlete, businessman, artist,or lover.

This is not mystical mumbo- jumbo.

If you see yourself as a great cabinet maker, you first see yourself crafting the end product. Then you reverse engineer your life to achieve. You do what you must do to achieve it. In so doing, you begin to actually become the master craftsman, you wish to become. And, in time, everything around you changes. Including your relationships, where you live, what you drive, your very waking hours and when you sleep. It all is

TRANSFORMED

All winners achieve in this manner. They see the end and dial back to get there. This is transformation, that is real, long lasting and of great value to your philosophy. Simply, competing makes life just a series of conflicts and games, and does alter who you are, except you may have earned more W's, but have you created the life you want for yourself?

The concept here is :

I will DECIDE where I want to COMPETE. I will WIN based upon my own values, and TRANSFORM myself to achieve my success.

And I will LIVE AS THOUGH I AM ALREADY THERE

This puts the idea that life is a game into a philosophical perspective that can be achieved

THE ZERO SUM GAME

Let's be clear, you can have a life philosophy, a Manosophy, and be competitive, fight for your dream and beliefs. And you may need to be tough on yourself, and those who stand in your way, want to harm you, take what is rightfully yours, and just plain want to beat down in a game, or at the job. But, you will have a direction and a goal which is ultimately to transform who you are to accomplish the fulfillment of the life you want.

There is a tendency is the unexamined life, so many of us have led, to believe that a loss is a victory for our competitors and devastating hit to who we are at that moment. The memories of grade school competitions, and the pain of coming home with a loss, or the emotional battering of high school coaches for any loss. There was rarely a respite, from a generation raised on the ZERO SUM GAME. A win for others suggests deep flaw in the losers. The motivation to win was often to alleviate the pain of loss, a purist definition of complex philosophy of the will to power and the influence of pleasure over pain.

The ZSG outlook is pervasive from man to man. It is a psychological club wielded to suppress our inner being, and drives the concept of gain, even in loss out of our consciousness. This outlook forces a self definition that defies actual achievement studies. Whether you look to politics, science, or sport, loss and failure serves as much to create great results as does winning alone. Lincoln, Edison, and the Babe failed as much as they won. Yet, their inner spirit and willfulness brought us an iconic President, scientific advancement after thousands of failed experiments; and, the ultimate home run hitter, in a sea of strike outs.

ZSG advocates contend it forces excellence, and hardiness, while striking almost cellular repulsion to losing. And it does do that in extremis. But, it also can destroy initiative, weaken desire to compete, or foster a loser mentality, when none should exist. Think about how pervasive this outlook is in our culture and weigh its benefits against the spirits it has destroyed. It is a way of approaching life that has high costs, if like most of us, you will fail and lose repeatedly; and, no one has an undefeated season in life.

As you reverse engineer your goals and seek transformation of your outlook and life mission, the ZSG loses its power over you. And those around you who believe it is a marker of a "real man" will also lose their grip over your self – esteem. This alone will set you a new and more powerful inner journey.

As always it is your choice. But your POP is enhanced if :
THE ZERO SUM GAME is NOT a GAME you PLAY.

OUTLOOK ON THE PEOPLE IN YOUR LIFE

So much of our outlook emanates from the outlook of those around us, especially our parents, or lack of them in our upbringing. The basis of our foundational optimism or pessimism often stems from our early life experiences as interpreted by our parents. It is common in most households for a mix of viewpoints to be in the atmosphere surrounding events. Often, in two parent homes, the outlooks may conflict. Single mother have substantial influence with their mono- view of life. Extended families offer bridges across generations that may conflict with current viewpoints.

You have heard these axioms that serve as world views or operating systems for family units.

Everything Happens for a Reason

They are getting theirs for sure, they don't give a damn about us

The Rich get Richer, the poor, poorer

Where is mine, I work my ass off and this is what I get?

Just keep your nose clean and work hard. Stay out of trouble.

Look at you, all Hat and No cattle

Whatever, you want just go for it. Work for it.

Nobody ever gave me something for nothing

If it is too good to be true, it's a lie

No one is going to give you life on a silver platter

Just do what makes you happy, life is too damn short

Do not waste your gifts, child. That's the greatest sin.

In most homes, this can be a confusing mix of concepts. Harsh from some adults, and encouraging from others. How resilient you are to these influences is often a subtle mix of experiences, early successes and failures, and your own genetic influences. No one knows exactly why a son emerges fearful and quiet, while the daughter is confident and self assured.

What we do know is that these influences can be altered by an active, aware, adult mind seeking to find their own outlook that fits their life game plan. We may be destined by our genetic code to be more like our father or mother, or grandfather in our essential essence. But, beyond that coding there are myriad variations that come from experiences, different results and circumstances, and mostly from an effort to recalculate your mindset and create an outlook on life that is of your design and no one elses.

INVENTORY OF INFLUENCERS

There are obvious people who can have enormous influence upon our outlook. It is worth reviewing their hold on your personal beliefs. This is certainly a difficult task, because it requires a certain honesty with yourself. This is an important assessment that need not be shared with anyone, but it will assist you as you navigate towards the POP you desire.

Use the following simple criteria to assess their influence on their outlook on life;

Apply these to parents, girlfriends, wife, bosses, and even to your best friends.

FACTORS

Are they usually upbeat and optimistic about life

Do they support you in efforts to find new pursuits, recreational and vocationally

Is their idea of a good life what you want?

Are they stuck in a pattern of seeing you as done with life choices?

Do they support your desire to find happiness, does it seem important to them?

Do parents conflict on view of life?

How important is religion or faith in their assessment of your direction?

Are they growing emotionally?

Do you feel they manipulate you to get what they want?

Are you ever the leader of events, ideas, gatherings.

Do your friends understand you?

If you exchange any one of them for another "model" would you

These are searching and difficult questions. Often, we never ask them, afraid that the answers will cause a crisis in confidence about those closest to us. There is no single person that will fulfill all our needs or serve to fully embrace your quest to develop a game plan of your own. They are helpers, lovers, and confidants who can be kindred spirits along the way. Not, any of them, not a single one is the reason you re not where you wish to be.

Even the most evil, misdirected parent cannot destroy the child. The most wayward wife cannot remove love from your heart; the most two faced friend cannot convince you that friendship does not have great value. Unless you let them. The power to change and transform is within you. Realize people in your life for what they are and what they contribute.

Then assess where they fit in philosophy, as you evolve. It is your decision, of what influence they will have, and how you approach and embrace them going forward.

So, you can

MAKE AN HONEST ASSESSMENT OF THE PEOPLE IN MY LIFE AS I PURSUE A PERSONAL OPERATING PHILOSOPHY

Getting What You Want in Life while following your Manosophy

As you develop your outlook, what you want to accomplish will become apparent and obvious. You will begin to see goals as achievable across a spectrum of long term and short term considerations. Usually the long term goals will be grandiose and require time and incremental gains; while short term opportunities will suggest shorter paths to accomplishment.

Running a marathon takes training, commitment to building endurance, and three to six months of devoted effort. Buying a rifle, requires,knowledge, some research and a strong desire to become a marksmen or sportsman. Yet, it takes little time to acquire the rifle, more to acquire the skills. And, some goals, are more celestial and require not only willfulness, but help from the "forces". Often men want to get married, have a family, and a good job.

This array of goals often begins, for most men, with the pursuit of a livelihood, where life then intercedes, due as much to being available and open to relationships, as through devoted planning. Yet, single minded goals do help drive energy and release the essential power we all have within us to accomplish, even the most insane or crazy pursuits. And often, these visions manifest themselves across a timeline that is different than we planned, or almost magically happen when we least expect the outcome.

But, none of it transpires unless there is a devotion to finding the right attitude and approach to these sought after goals and results. You can have a buoyant,optimistic outlook and still not reach results. Often this is the direct result of self- imposed restraints that are based upon fear of success and /or failure; unwillingness to do the work of planning; pure laziness; or settling into a routine that provides you with a modicum of success and profits but will not take you out of your comfort zone to the true transformation that finally frees you to the transcendent life you actually desire.

Different approaches are often required to reach goals, and they should be seen as a toolbox of approaches, rather than as definitions of your essential way of doing things. Often one approach, needs to combine with another to move towards goals effectively, and with a certain speed.

Every Goal Requires a Plan

Every outcome you require needs to have a simple plan of attack that is in sync with your POP. It need take long to write it out:

> What outcome do I want?
> What steps do I take to get there?
> What resources do I bring to accomplish the tasks?
> Do I need to enlist others?
> How long with this take?
> How do I measure if I got the outcome I desired?

There is nothing you can desire that cannot be diagrammed in this manner. This works for short and long term goals, and the most serious to frivolous. Here is a serious example:

> Goal: I want to go to law school
> Enroll in Ivy League School
> Create good grades and then transfer in junior year to pre-law
> Use contacts and references
> 7 years at accelerated rate
> Law degree is most important result- from where less valid
> A more mundane example:
> Goal: party for Josh who is 21
> Friends gather to celebrate
> Car pools and booking in Las Vegas
> Delegate transportation and guest lists
> Three weeks to date
> Did everyone show up and enjoy themselves, and no one gets arrested

It may seem that taking the time to plan, is obsessive and overdone. And, certainly some matters are done so quickly they require no actual pre thought. But, most decisions are better planned this way. It keeps you awake, in the present, and allows you to determine OUTCOMES that are intended and,even, unintended.

Approaches towards goals run across a range of techniques. Sometimes you will need to be tough and direct. Others require listening, empathy, and stillness before you can go forward. And most often you will get further as a collaborator than on your own. Different goals require a combination of approaches, including being solitary, hard headed, stubborn, and willful. You can't always get what you want through collaboration, sometimes, your singular vision must be followed, regardless of how coarse, crazy or anti- social it may appear.

You just must select the approach (tools), you need to reach a goal based upon your instincts, who you are, and what your philosophy tells you is right.

But, the basic underlying foundation of any approach when not dealing with a flock of bastards is:

BE KIND, NO EXCUSES

As modern men are we currently inclined to be individualists, create value, and pioneer new ideas and in so doing be strong representatives of ourselves?

It certainly seems that we are pulled into another direction, where we are pushed to conform, yield to others, and be quiet to the mainstream psychology. Men are more damned for aggression, foresight, and toughness. Often, the modern man is seen as compliant, afraid of his spouse or girlfriend, wary of taking sides, and unable to pursue what he wants.

This is not the man with a developed POP, that allows for self –realization and a transformation to become what you are meant to be. Philosophy empowers with a view of self that is rugged and individual. This uniqueness is what characterized the men who moved West to Manifest the Destiny of America. It is the men who built the country through the industrial revolution, and launched us into being a world power. Teddy Roosevelt called them, "men in the arena", who desired engagement, battled adversity, and enjoyed the competition of ideas. It is this dynamic of engagement, wrestling with thoughts and gnashing out results that defines men. And this is true on the playing field, the lab, and Wall Street.

There is no philosophy of man that does not find a robust, energetic spirit, unfettered by others, whether government, wives, or parents, as the essential quality that releases the very stuff of a transformative life.

Whether you find this theme in the biographies of great men, or even in the mega – fiction of Ayn Rand, in her Atlas Shrugged, the reality is unavoidable. Action based upon self interest, and an planned pursuit of goals defines a man's life philosophy, it is there for the taking. Yet, so many fail to see it. So many hope life will just evolve and they will get what they desire through the magic of fate or faith.

AMOR FATI

Ancient Roman thinkers believed, in their superstitious and pagan times, that the Gods had a plan for most men. That the "fates" as they called them could not be altered, each man from his station in life, his family, had a circumstances pre- determined. And it as therefore, not for a man to rail against his destiny, but, to embrace his fate, and enjoy his life the best could, knowing his fate could only be altered by the Gods.

Thus, embrace your fate, or in Latin, AMOR FATI

It is probably hard to believe that centuries later, in this modern, secular time that anyone would still let their lives be lived by fate or fortune. Millions of men approach their life philosophy as though they cannot alter the results of their upbringing, geographic location, race, or ethnic origin. It is the philosophy of throwing your destiny to others, living their plan for you. It is a soul crushing life, even if you are born to wealth, possess great physical beauty or have gifts that are inherent.

It is still the case that the axiom about life holds force:

THE UNEXAMINED LIFE IS NOT WORTH AS MUCH AS THE LIFE EXAMINED

This does not mean that all the planning, and exertion will always result in the outcome your desire. For, the "forces" do exist. These aspects of what surrounds us that is not seemingly in our control. To Star War fans, THE FORCE is a God like essence that offer good an opportunity to triumph. There is a good force of the Jedi Knights and, the opposing forces of darkness. It is always present, and only needs to be accessed to assist the Jedi. It is strong at times, and weak at others.

Poet and everyman, Charles Bukowski often blamed the forces for his life battles. The woman he wined and dined who screwed him over, the father who was absent, the too many beers, he consumed. It was more often the fates and the forces that set him off, but also saved him from a life as a drunken poet, overlooking a skid row street in West Los Angeles.

He embraced the fates.

Neo found the essential question of life revealed, after

he swallowed a pill from Morpheus. He could have gone blue pill and continued the unexamined life; but, he took red instead. He found that the reality he believed in was, but, a sham. The Matrix ruled a created,cyber world, and reality could be found, only if the human spirit prevailed.

These battles over what is real, and true, and fate is on going. Some deep thinkers still contend that we have but a particle of free will, and that our genetic make up and the universe has us set for what we can achieve or become. But, an outlook based upon that still does not limit what you can decide to do for yourself.

While, there is no question that "shit happens", we can embrace the assault and move forward with our outlook intact. Our founding fathers believed that there was an eternal force that created all of this, they were Deists. But, Jefferson also contended that once the clock was created, the clockmaker retreated to let us create our own world, even as the clock ticked by on our lives. So, the fate and the forces would always be there, but we could rail against them or capitulate.

Leaving us with this for our outlook:

THE FORCES AND FATES MAY DISRUPT, BUT THEY WILL NOT DETERMINE MY DESTINY

SOME UNIQUE OUTLOOKS YOU MAY NOT HAVE CONSIDERED

Rocky Balboa

By the sixth movie, Sylvester Stallone has taken his doppleganger, Rocky Balboa back to Philadelphia, as the essential champion returned to the regular life. He has lost his life companion and wife, Adrian, and his son, now a financial guru, has lost his close affiliation with his father. Rocky and his brother in law Pauley return to his old haunts, and touchingly remember the early years. The pain that comes with the nostalgia is almost paralyzing.

Rocky is adrift, and very much alone with his memories. His son needs to stand up to a boss that is asking him to alter his values to survive in his business. He meets his father on the street, on a bitter cold night

ROCKY

It's life, you know. Its not about how many times you get knocked down. That doesn't make you a champion. Its about how many times you get up!

A succinct outlook, to be sure:

LIFE IS ABOUT TAKING IT. GOING FOR IT. AND GETTING UP. FIGHT THE FORCES. FIGHT BACK. YOUR DESTINY CAN ONLY BE FOUND IF YOU NEVER EVER GIVE UP

Master Your Mat

George Leonard was an Aikido master. He also created the spiritual getaway, at a place called Esalen, yoga, meditation, Zen and the Martial Arts all emanated from this sensei, master. His book Mastery, and Aikido are powerful, concise looks at the application of Zen and martial arts to a life philosophy.

His primary outlook is that whatever you seek in life, you must simply OWN YOUR MAT, or be totally devoted to where you are, and what you desire fully, with any tentative moves. And he offered a formula for attacking any life problem or goal.

It has these elements:

Center Yourself: prepare for what is ahead. Marshall your energy.

Assess: what is the challenge, how much force do I need to prevail

Blend: move towards your goal or adversary, summon their energy within

Attack: move with all your power and force, and be devastating

Retreat: step away to review your attack, and center again

Adapt: If the force and energy was unsuccessful, find another avenue

Begin again until goal is reached or threat destroyed

This approach can be applied to any problem. And for him, the attack was always soft, flowing, and using the energy of the obstacle to achieve maximum results.

The Mystic

And finally, this mystical and bizarre true tale of a mystic from Ethiopia.

In the 1930's in Egypt, there lived a black, Ethiopian Jew, named Abdullah.

He was a rabbi and mystic, who taught early Christian and Jewish thought. But, he was also seen as a seer, who could tell the future. He advised believers in the occult, predicted life changes for believers from Nazi Germany, and Rudolph Hess to American Neville Goddard.

It would be Goddard who fashioned an entire self help philosophy from Abdullah's teachings. Fundamentally the Ethiopian believed that the only true outlook and philosophy stemmed from an obvious, but ancient belief.

YOU CAN BECOME WHATEVER YOU WANT TO BE. BUT, WE MUST DECIDE UPON THAT AIM. LEAVE OUR OTHER LIFE. AND, OCCUPY THE NEW LIFE.

Or in Neville's terms: You Attract what you Believe to be True.

Simply it is a philosophy of beliefs. You decide who you want to become .You take steps to achieve. But you ACT as IF you are Already THERE. It is, in fact, this belief and action that rockets you where you want to be. Suddenly you dress the way you want to be, your speech changes, your friends change, you are transformed, precisely because, you have decided to vacate the old you, and eventually the old psyche and replace yourself.

It is a bold operation. Neville preached it across America.

It required a real commitment to a transformation of the soul. It was harsh, but its simplicity was powerful

LIVE AS THOUGH YOU ARE THERE... AND THAT YOU SHALL BE

Neville's brand of self- realization became the foundation of generations of self help guru's from Dwayne Dwyer to Tony Robbins. The basics being the same and valid for any philosophy. Change Your Thinking. Develop a Plan. Take Action.

What Are You Prepared to DO?

Select a viewpoint; write out your thoughts; what fits your developing world view? Act out a few of these and experiment with how they make you feel.

CHAPTER III

What Is Your Code

"You can't handle the truth!...Son, we live in a world that has walls. I have a greater responsibility than you can possibly fathom...You don't want the truth... You need me on that wall. We use words like honor, CODE, loyalty...we use these words as the backbone to a life spent defending something."

Colonel Nathan R. Jessup

For this Marine officer testifying in court, in the film, A Few Good Men, Jack Nicholson offers a stunning speech about the way he operates in the world, and the code he lives by regardless of the consequences. Writer Aaron Sorkin captures the essence of this officers sense of his standards of right and wrong in disciplining a young Marine.

In our lives, our outlook determines how we see the world and those around us. A Code is how we act, how we conduct ourselves as we go through each day. These codes can be imposed by an organization, a family, a religion, or our own social circle. But, there are fundamental aspects to most codes that seek to offer a way of conducting yourself, how you treat others, and how to deal with challenges in life.

Manosophy is based upon a type of man, who develops a code that allows for the expression of inner spirit and encourages the growth of a man's potential. This often is characterized as the CODE OF THE WARRIOR, that emanates from the ancient Tibetan translation of Pawo or "brave". Bravery drives the warrior code, since it is an essential element in fighting the forces that challenge a man in life.

Warrior is not just a man with a Samurai sword or a rifle. There are codes for men who defend freedom and a way of life through military might. But, most men can be warriors of their own spirits that have codes as rigorous and purposeful as that of Colonel Jessup.

Codes let you find your way through day to day challenges, and when needed, to face issue that force you out of your comfort zone with grace, and power. Codes offer the very definition of right and wrong, or an ethical pathway for action. The Warrior Code encourages honesty, resilience, courage, and even a sense of lightness and perspective on all that happens, regardless of its severity or life changing outcome.

Living by a code does require a degree of discipline and honesty. The reason we have codes is to offer a guidance system as we go through our days. Codes can be a simple as, "I will dress appropriately for any situation, wear shoes, and a shirt in public. Not use a curse word in every sentence.

Stop saying f…king. "or they can be more grandiose," I will not murder, I will not steal, I will not bear false witness."

The classic code through the ages comes from Moses' trek up Mt. Sinai. It was part of larger bond between the Hebrew God, Jehovah, and his people, it created a covenant between God and his people. Follow this code and you shall be bound to me forever. Thus, the Ten Commandments became part of all Judeo- Christian culture. Nothing about them that is difficult to understand or accomplish. But, as in most religious codes, they spend as much time on commitment to God as to ourselves. For believers in Christ, the code is even more direct; believe in God, the father; believe that I have come to earth to absorb your sins; and do unto others what you have them do unto you. And that if you live this code, you will have everlasting life.

Religious codes often offer an incentive for following them. For Christians it is heaven and everlasting life; for Judaism it is a well lived life based upon repairing the world and ourselves; for Buddhists, it is living on the right path, and managing struggle and suffering, in search of a higher consciousness, Nirvana. For believers in Islam, it is a well lived life that honors the Prophet Muhammed and offers a place in a heaven and afterlife for believers. Each faith has its own reward system, but each also requires a commitment to a certain WAY of living, based upon a code.

The warrior code can be derived from an eclectic amalgam of precepts gleaned from a number of codes. At the end of the chapter, you can develop your own code, that fits your beliefs and desires. Having a personal code, to complement your outlook, helps form a personal operating philosophy that composes a unified Manosophy.

Foundational Codes
MARINES- the Ultimate Warrior Code
Unit, Corps, God, Country

For a Marine the ultimate commitment is to his fellow Marines. The cohesion of the unit is the building block of everything that makes them effective fighting men. They are prepared to give their lives for the cause of American freedom, through the code of caring for the other men with whom the serve. So, while their lives matter, it is as important to instill and protect the life of the man next to you in battle. The result is you are never alone, in life, battle, or death. You will never be left behind, nor will your compatriots.

This unit consciousness is very powerful, in any tightly held value driven social network, including your family or loved ones. It is essentially that group that you will defend at all costs, including death, as part of your code. It is the most essential requirement of a code, who will you die for, or not.

The Corps is a commitment to the larger unit, the association with something, larger than themselves that possesses the themes that allow the unit to function. This may be the values of your profession, employer, or long term history of an institution you revere or have committed to through your life. Larger institutions have history, a record of defending core values and have codes that have made them successful.

Men who are trained and mentally prepared to sacrifice their lives in battle, rarely have no belief system in a higher power. Whether is a traditional God, or an unformed belief, agnostics before the bullets fly, are praying after the triggers are pulled. There is a calm that provokes an inner knowing, for men who can still summon someone to reference as all hell breaks loose. Few warrior codes have no higher power to believe in in some way.

No Marine fights for the purity of the battle or the emotional charge that comes with surviving a fire fight. They are fighting for something. That is freedom, liberty, and the rights guaranteed by our country. The unique and exceptional historic place that America has in protecting and fostering certain unalienable rights is the ultimate cause. Everything that America is about,runs through each Marine. On a cellular level, these freedoms and rights are the driving force behind the success and essence of being a Marine, the true Warrior spirit.

Marines own the following codes;

Never lie
Never Cheat
Never Steal
Have Courage
Master your Fear
Be Committed to the Mission

And if necessary as a result of battle:

Be prepared to give my life
Never surrender
Resist if Captured
Name and Rank
Believe in America
Be of Faith in God

It is code with a certain starkness that reflects the reality of what a Marine may face. Still, much of it is transcendent, to all men. And it is a code that stays with these men, in service and out. The phrase, "Once a Marine, always a Marine" comes from this code, in is indelible and unshakeable.

How fortunate is America that these Marines exist and protect us and our values, so we have the freedom to construct our own life code.

BUSHIDO

The Japanese warrior was embodied in the fearsome, Samurai, who was highly trained in fighting as well as the way of Zen and Buddhism. They also pledged a fealty to their Lord and landowners, while also developing in the arts of painting, poetry, and gardening. Romantics in modern culture often depict them as warrior/poets. Men of substantial killing capability but possessed of feelings for nature and their surroundings.

The Samurai code was a composite of Zen, Buddha, Confucianism, but was embodied in the foundational code of BUSHIDO, or Way of the Warrior. The precepts of Bushido are still accessible in our modern world. They are neither quaint, nor esoterically foreign.

Their actual fighting methods are encased in forms of martial arts that are practiced in modern day Kendo and Aikido, but the philosophy of the code requires no special training to achieve.

Rectitude

It is a belief that there is always an obvious right and

wrong path. Ethics is not a complex nor winding path. The warrior can often easily see what is the proper direction, and should always select the right way and be prepared to defend the consequences.

Courage

Doing what is right and required is not easy for most warriors. Everyone has their own needs and desires. It takes courage to overcome these personal, or ego driven forces and select the perfect action. Life problems emerge when, the warrior cannot meet his obligations to carry out a task in the proper direction. And, if in battle, a lack of courage can lead to indecision, which in hesitation can be fatal.

Benevolence

Possessing skills as a warrior presents a strong force on events and those surrounding the Samurai. But having power, might, and influence does not allow the misuse of these attributes over others who do not possess them. People who are not foes, should be treated with kindness and offerings to assist them where needed. A great warrior is also an open, and caring person. Kindness is as critical to this code as is uncompromising lethal force on enemies.

Respect

Bushido requires that people be treated according to their accomplishments. Everyone is not known for their warrior skills, and must be shown respect for what they have accomplished, whether as a mother, scholar, or clerk. Treating everyone as a person of value and as a contributor instills a feeling of nobility for the warrior.

Honesty

Easy to list, but very challenging to achieve. Often dishonesty is used as a convenient dodge from dealing with problems. It can excuse away life challenges and dilemmas, or, worse forestall decisions. Honesty takes courage, but strikes at rectitude. They are bound together, the right way is always the way of honesty.

Humor

The most stern warrior cultivates a sense of humor, about himself and his situations. Often it is the most dire circumstance that requires humor to offer the relief, before one must go forward. Especially in the heart of darkness, humor can lift a spirit or lighten the moment. Humor inserted naturally, buoys the spirit, and cleanses the warrior for right action. Humor makes for hardy warriors, who gain perspective in the most difficult places and times. Even when all seems lost, or at cross purposes, humor can help.

Loyalty

In Bushido, this part of the code was the driving force of existence. In the feudal system, the Lord was the central focus of all activity. Yet, warriors were more than connected to the Lord, they also were devoted to each other and their village. They fought for each other, and were prepared to die for family, village and the Lord. And they expected rewards in the afterlife, for their efforts, including re-incarnation.

KING ARTHUR and the Knights of The Roundtable

This is a code that is part fable and the reality of the Crusades. There was no Camelot, no Arthur, no Sir Lancelot. But, there was a code of chivalry that emerged in the time of knights and Kings. Arthur was an Englishman who expelled the Saxons, and he had a roundtable of knights who observed a way of conduct that was based upon feudal realities, to protect the King and property, and, to fight to defend England from all invaders.

Chivalry began as defense of "horsemanship" and the proper carrying of animals and the warrior code of a swordsman. By the time of the Crusades, chivalry came to embody a code of conduct with its own foundational elements:

Military skills

Finely honed use of implements of war and horsemanship. The code was devoted to the swift and absolute defeat of any enemy.

Bravery

Willingness to fight, against any odds. Refusal to yield in battle and in pursuit of goals for the King.

Generosity

The spoils of battle are to be divided, accordingly, but not denied to those in most need including the vanquished

Piety

These battles and, indeed, life are done under the scrutiny of a Christian God and Christ himself. Everything done was for the glory of Christendom.

Courtesy towards Women

The classic Camelot measure of manners towards women. Women celebrated, treated well, and offered special treatment based upon gender. Clearly a view of the times, that objectified women, and gave them secondary status.

Chivalry as a code fit its time, unified warriors, was more centered on protection of property and King than upon self development and an inner power.

BUDDHISM

The outlook of this code requires no formal worship of deity. It presents a theory of life and how one can cope with the vagaries of existence. It is essentially a way of conducting yourself to reduce the struggle and suffering that Buddha felt all men encounter. Of course, the full study and commitment to being a Buddhist requires ritual, and reflection as do other faiths, but none of that is required to understand the essential code of the faith.

Suffering

All men will suffer, as they become attached to certain outcomes. Causes of suffering are many including, wealth, relationships, material possessions, and our need to cherish these things and feelings. No man can expect a life free of these bumps and bruises, they will come. But, the level of suffering and the inevitability of that experience can be reduced, deflected and foster transformation, if you follow THE EIGHTFOLD PATH

RIGHT Understanding

Realizing that suffering will occur and that the so called Four Noble Paths will help. The main point being that DUKKHA (suffering) is an essential part of life and Right action help end it.

Right Speech

Do not lie, no backbiting or slander

Right Action

Honesty, no stealing, no adultery

Right Work

Select work that fits your sense of purpose. Do no harm to others through work

Right Effort

Put your will behind efforts to improve the world and yourself

Right Mindfulness

Always be alert to the present. Cherish the current moment. Be awake

Right Concentration

You become and achieve what you focus upon. What you select is what you get

Right Thought

Thinking of others not just yourself

Right understanding

See things as they actually are, not as you wish them to be. Stop pretending and acknowledge what is actual.

These precepts like the others seem on their surface to be obvious. And they are not complex, but, realizing the path to Enlightenment is for Buddhists a life long journey. This is because there is a gap between what we know is the road or path, and whether or not we are prepared to follow it dutifully. Having a code requires such a pursuit, and must be a code that you can understand, and adopt, so it becomes a part of your every breath and action.

AWAKENING YOUR CODE

All codes believe in the power of the future. There is always the value of this moment, but a code offers insight into what a future will hold for us. Following a code brings order to the everyday, but, also informs the next moment. Understanding yourself and the "way" of your life, enables you to be a person imbued with the rising sun. You are about evolution, brightness, and transformation.

You develop a way of talking and walking tall that suggests a person with purpose and gravitas. You are less quick to speak, ramble, and force your views upon others; you are not argumentative, but firm in opinion and always prepared to act to achieve your beliefs.

This all comes with a self –realized code that propels you towards your goals.

Might your code consider these factors:

HONESTY

Be true to your values and speak the truth,always

BRAVERY

You are not afraid to step forward and help, even if you are in danger

COURAGE

You will not retreat from challenges that take you out of your comfort zone.

KINDNESS

When you see the opportunity you will all life stations with kindness

HUMOR

You realize that lightness in spirit is tool that elevates your very being. Without you existence is darkened

WARRIOR

This requires a pause. This is the heart of a life code. Most of us rarely have to face the question raised here. What will we defend? What will we die to protect? Is it our loved ones; our faith; our country; our freedoms.

It may be all of these things. And it is likely we really do not know the answer until confronted with the actual circumstance. But it seems worthy of thought, somehow. It tests our inner GPS.

Or is just as likely it starts and ends with self – preservation and the innate will to survive.

You will fight, and indeed, die for certain principles and beliefs. And, will protect those you love,or pledge to protect, with any means necessary.

NOT LIE, CHEAT, STEAL, OR MURDER

You adopt these ancient codes of the Ten Commandments.

SAY YES

You look for opportunities to be engaged in life, new pursuits, and opportunities to meet new people and ideas

ALWAYS BE IMPROVING

You realize that only way to transform your life is to commit to improving what needs change. If you are not improving you are losing.

CONSTANT LEARNING CURIOSITY

You explore new ideas, research unknown areas, and are curious about ideas, people and concepts.

NOT BE HABIT DRIVEN

You examine all your habits. You review your look, eating, diet, speech patterns to improve them, so they serve your long term goals. You are prepared to alter any habit that retards your transformation to the man you want to become.

This effort to create your own code, is about giving you coping strategies that will inform your life purpose. You want a "way" and you can create it, without a guru, a dojo, or an on line course. There is no reason to be lost upon a "sea of harshness", as defined by Zen thinkers. This code will rocket you immediately into a direction and process of self – realization that will immediately fuel your creation of a game plan for your life.

WHAT ARE YOU PREPARED TO DO?

What code fits you best

What are the elements of your code

Can you write down your code

Create a calendar for achievement

Live the code for thirty days and see if it works for you

What amendments does your code need to become part of you?

TAMING THE BEAST OF ANGER

"No one man, or woman, lover, wife, adversary, opponent, enemy or outside force can destroy your hopes, dreams, and plans faster and with more finality than action that comes from a moment of ANGER"

All men have this common emotion. Most can learn to control it enough so it will not destroy or alter the course of a life. But it can.

One burst of emotion can go from a benign outburst of road rage to chronic rage that becomes murderous. The line between the one and the other is remarkably thin. This emotion comes from a place as ancient as our beginning evolutionary survival mechanisms. The biology of anger is not complex. Two almond size structures sit before the prefrontal cortex that provides us with judgment. These amygdala are our "threat" center. Something triggers it a threat, a fear, an affront, and neurotransmitters begin to spew into our system. First, catecholamine releases immediate energy getting us ready to respond; then your heart rate speeds up, blood leaves your gut and goes to your arms, legs and fists.

You become focused upon the target of your angst, and adrenaline and non- adrenaline flows. You are ready to fight, or more likely speak your mind, wave your fist, hit a wall, or pose serious threats.

Usually, the prefrontal cortex will catch you before you overreact, but not always. If you deploy no anger management techniques, you can make a life altering statement, choice or move in an instant and alter the entire course of your life.

And unfortunately, even with calming techniques, it takes time, many hours, sometimes, days for you to return to normal levels. And in this period, some other trigger that has nothing to do at all with the original stimulus will elicit another anger episode, that seems out of proportion to you and others. This secondary episode is often as capable of damage as the first, because it holds no obvious context for the perceived overreaction.

Anger is the apex emotion of our dark side.

Here are some common anger scenarios;

Obvious threat

You are confronted by someone who is gleefully doing something that pleases them but irritates you, like playing loud music after 2am. Or, a lout is cursing at public space, and annoying everyone around them.

You are angry because this is self absorbed behavior and not acceptable to your norms.

Impending Attack

You are challenged in a road rage incident, and believe the driver is out to physically harm you. You prepare to flee or defend yourself

Shamed

You go to a dinner but are dressed inappropriately. Your friends did not tell you what was the proper attire. You are fit to be tied in rage.

Powerless

You make a presentation at work that was approved by your supervisor. But, when you offer it, your best work is rejected by the senior Vice President. You are angry because you have no voice in the final decision, and were misled.

Injustice

Your son has made the football team, and is expected to play Varsity quarterback. The coach, however, is going to start another boy. He is the son of the schools' major financial contributor. This is unfair on every level, and you are about to give the coach and the President a piece of your mind.

Surprised

You attend a family dinner, in a distant city. You are looking forward to the exchange with people you have not seen in years. Yet, you are surprised to see Uncle Harry is also there, a man you blamed for the death of your father's sister. No one told you, and you are angry with the host and others.

Lies

You dearly love your teenage daughter, but she told you

she going to the library to study for the last four weeks and you find, she spent the time making out with her boyfriend. You have anger about the lie, and never liked the boyfriend, and she knows it.

Loss of Love

Your wife of many years, tell you she wants a divorce. An investment of love, and time is threatened, and you only have anger to transmit, as you get the news.

Loss of Life

Your son is shot in a drive by shooting and you are in court for the preliminary hearing. The rage is building, and you are about to explode in the courtroom.

Security

A co worker has told your boss that you are not living up to your potential. You want to kill her, for threatening your job security.

All of the scenarios have the same core, which emanates from a deep sense of displeasure, dislike and irritation. Each requires different skills to control, but none will find resolution of long term value, from a burst of anger. This does not mean that anger is not a valid emotion, or should not be displayed or released at times. But, knowing you triggers and how you can respond lessens the probability that your reaction will harm your game plan.

Sometimes this anger comes from being too hard on yourself. You know you can sink that jump shot, return that serve, or hit under pressure. But, the more anger you express, the less likely you are to accomplish the task. In fact, the harder you grip the bat, the more likely you are to go into a slump. The way out and towards success is actually, relaxation and review, not anger and self defeating comments or actions.

ANGER CONTROLS

There are many anger management books as there are self help gurus. They all offer the same essential formula. Identify the trigger, do not react immediately, and work on the triggers to avoid getting agitated. These suggestions do work, of course, but may not provide the type of triage needed for men caught in situations where anger might arise.

The first diagnostic is to determine which trigger is getting to you. Is it shame, injustice, surprise, or self inflicted anger from not performing at your best. Can you get enough space between the incident and your analysis of the triggering emotion. Except for direct attacks there usually is an interval where some thought can be applied. But even, when confronted and a response is needed, our formula from Aikido applies. Center and assess, before you blend with your opponent and stage an attack.

How big an issue is this affront? And what is a proportional response ? Often our anger based outbursts seem much more robust than the incident would suggest.

It is often best to be silent, and only express yourself once you have heard out the offender or attempted through silence and breathing to calm yourself. And remember, the only to be in control to be

OUTCOME SPECIFIC

What is it you want from this encounter? Do want to hurt the person, emotionally or even physically? Do want to just have them know you are hurt and angry? Is this a one time only encounter or does it suggest chronic issues?

Knowing what outcome you desire, gives you back the power of the destination of the encounter being in your hands again.

When you do speak, attempt to be non judgmental and open minded, so you call disarm the opponent. Use I phrases and refrain from accusations or "you" statements. Get the person to understand you are attempting to understand and with hold your anger.

However, you should always be honest and state clearly what is wrong that triggers this debate. Decide if the outcome you require, is best served by being forceful or more relaxed about your concerns.

Sometimes there is no remedy. Then you state your concerns directly, and move on. Debates of some length usually exacerbate the trigger and rarely resolve it.

AFTER THE TRIGGER EVENT

Once the initial shock and trigger has passed, you must be alert to the after effect of the flow of hormones through your body and brain. The flight or fight mechanism is deeply ingrained genetically, and requires time to play out. And, any other lesser trigger may come and offer a reverberating response that will suddenly overtake you.

Often, we find that a colleague or friend gets extraordinarily angered over a usually benign event, like a spilled cup of coffee. But the reaction is volcanic. Often the anger we see is not about anything we witness. And for deeply troubled folks, chronic rage emerges with frightening frequency.

After the trigger, activity matters. Exercise, walking, deep breathing, meditation can all assist in the release of potent hormones and neurotransmitters. Humor is another booster of better chemistry. Approaching the incident with a sense of humor can create an emotional distance from it and any consequences or fall out.

IT IS ALWAYS THERE

This flight or fight response is always within us. It is part of our survival code.

At times it drives us to overcome fear, and to act in the face of enormous adversity. These chemicals and our biology exist to protect us from harm, verbal and physical. It is not our purpose to avoid it, dismiss it, and over control this base emotion.

It is instead to understand its origins, assess their grip on us, and respond according to the outcomes we seek in any situation. By being alert to the emotion within us, we have some hope of containing,the enormous power Anger has to destroy us.

With a good outlook, our code, and an understanding of what can threaten our game plan for life, we turn to other forces wrought by others that we must have the courage to fight.

What are you Prepared to DO?

What are your trigger points? Can you identify when you lost it and why? Can you learn to control anger when it erupts?

CHAPTER IV

The Four Horsemen Shame, Approval, Guilt, Fear

"Hell in my opinion is never finding your true self and never living your own life or knowing who you are."

John Bradshaw

This inner journey to reveal who we are and what we want for ourselves has obstacles that we place in front of ourselves and those thrust upon us by others. Often it is those closest to us that offer the most formidable challenges. They come from most often the women in our lives, a loving,but protective spouse or mother, and,even, sisters and co- workers. These are blockades of emotional energy that can be used by men or women, to protect their power over you and delay for years your progress to self- realization of your game plan for your life.

They come like horsemen across the road of your life,

providing powerful emotional forces that literally scare the hell out of you. Borrowing from the Book of Revelations, where the four horsemen are the anti-Christ on the white horse; War on the red; Famine on the black; and Death on the pale horse. Each guarantees the end of man, and the eventual coming of a new age. For us, the horseman also signal the destruction of something, in our case, the development of our personal operating philosophy.

They ride over us as Shame, Approval, Guilt and Fear. They are obvious obstacles, experienced by us all, but, no less powerful and destructive. And when wielded by people around us, they are destroyers of our self-esteem and worthiness. But while they will be brought against men for all time, they do not have to penetrate our self image and retard our movement forward.

SHAME

This is wielded as a controlling tool, it suggests that you have taken some action that is not "worthy". It is about what YOU have done and you should be ashamed of the action. Often the action is not a matter of shame at all, but, the person that wishes to control your behavior employs shame as a weapon. When taken to extremes, you can develop a sense of being inadequate, and all self evaluations make you believe you are "bad".

These feelings, often ingrained in youth, or by loved ones later in life, can lead to feelings of being not wanted, worthless, or rejected. They are imposed as others seek to control your behavior or actions. It is a powerful way to create a mechanism inside of man that acts as a barrier to control actions. Actions that you may find objectionable or outside of your own code of ethics will be obvious to you. But, shame will not be the best way to control your actions. You can decide that the action was not appropriate and remediate your behavior without feeling worthless or inadequate .

Shaming is designed to make you feel humiliated, stupid, or worse, publically shame you as others watch. These experiences say far more about the person who is using shame as a controlling tool than on you. Often the shame user is revealing a flaw in their personality, or upbringing that is now being passed on to you. If you allow it, it will damage you, or at least, delay your journey to create a game plan for your life. Shame is exactly about denying you your life plan, in favor of the guidelines of others. It is precisely their plan that they want you to follow, or how you fit into their story.

What you desire or wish to pursue is damned by their own narrowly focused life script. This dominance of a mother, or loved one over you can severely damage your self image and must be fought at all costs. It requires an awareness of how shame is being used by others to MANIPULATE your feelings and harness your emotions in a negative manner. This identification requires a basic awareness of how others are critiquing your actions, and desires. You will know if what you did was in sync with your developing philosophy and code. If it was not, it was a mistake or an error in judgment, but, there is no reason to feel or be shamed by it. You are not useless or worthless, if you err, but only human and finite.

John Bradshaw spent a life studying the roots of shame in families. He fought his own alcoholism and shame based upbringing. He found entire family units based on shame based discipline and table talk. The result was generations of family life passed along, fostering shame used as a punishment, fostering shunning, and even creating dangerously anti- social personalities. Children who are shamed, raise children in shame based environments, this results, especially for men in reaction to such control, including addiction to ease the pain of feeling inadequate, abusive and harassing behavior towards women, and overwhelming self doubt .

Often men who are subject to shame as a control tool of their behavior, become arrogant, grandiose, thin skinned towards criticism, and are classic narcissists. Some develop hyper vigilant personalities that blame everyone else for mistakes and errors and refuse to see problems with their own choices. And they can lack empathy for others. Fortunately, these more extreme traits are ingrained at this level in few of us, but, we all share some fear of rejection and inadequacy.

As adults, we are often able to overcome some elements of shame based direction. But, it is around us, especially emerging in close relationships. To realize our own game plan, shame must be identified and compartmentalized so it does not destroy our inner progress.

Fighting Shame

What did you do?

The essential tool for awareness is the examination of the act that is in question. Was this something that you should not have done, pursued or accomplished. Did it fit within your own code?

What was the reaction of the person involved?

Often shame is brought by others, not the individual touched by your actions. Assess the impact of your actions on that person, not the shamming person.

Who is the accuser ?

What is the actual motivation of the person wielding the hammer of shame. What is their goal, is it to harm you, hold you back, or control you? Rarely does someone who uses shame hold your best interests at heart. It is more often their ego needs that are at stake and their goals that are protected.

Honest assessment

Regardless of shame, you still must own the incident. Was it right that you went out mid –week when you needed to study/ Was it proper that you dated your best friends ex / Should you have spent the morning golfing and not at a dance recital?

These assessments do have value. You can stay your course, only if you are prepared to be honest about your actions and the consequences they may bring about as well. You should do this not to feel insecure or worthless, but, instead that actions outside your game plan and code do not serve your purpose.

You note the error, take action with anyone you may have damaged or emotionally hurt, and resolve to move on.

APPROVAL

This is a more subtle obstacle, but is commonly found, not only in a family setting, but predominately in the workplace. As workplaces are often led by women, this is a tool often employed, and can powerfully influence your self- development. Women use leadership tactics that are often similar to men, but the creation of circles or cliques of approval is a mechanism often used to control and direct behavior in men.

You may believe you are doing a meritorious job, but others may believe you are either uncooperative, or lagging. Certainly, others may feel you do not "fit in." And a boss will make you feel isolated or as a satellite to the main functioning groups. This type of control is effective since we all seek to be part of the tribe at work. The inner circle of the boss is especially enticing.

Women who manage by clique, have adopted this behavior from generations of male dominated organizations that opted away from their inclusion. Yet, whether dominated by a woman executive or a man, they are a lousy way to lead. People feel excluded, and will not perform at an optimum level. If you feel less than equal, there is more incentive to retreat and hide your creativity and skills than be expansive with them.

And the fallacy of forcing a man to want to opt into group is that smart and resilient men find their own groups, and often they proceed productively in defiance of the ruling elite or cliques. Any situation that requires you to constantly seek approval before you can move forward, where you have no sphere of influence of your own, is toxic to the growth of your game plan and operating philosophy.

Further, if at work or in relationships, you feel forced outside of decision- making, or engaged in spending time, going through artificially created loops, to gain entry, you are being played, manipulated and controlled by the group leader either boss or loved one.

It takes courage to fight back against a clique or inner circle approval scheme. The instinct is to join the group, hoping for power and some self control of your destiny. And you my penetrate that group, and gain approval. But, it will always be tenuous. There will always be an even smaller inner circle, the elites have circles within circles. And, the reality is, as difficult as it may seem, those who lead by approval mechanism will never admit you as one of them.

How then to :

COPE WITH APPROVAL

Value of being in inner circle

What gains you entry to the group? Are their values the same as yours? Will you be more productive or improve if inside the group?

Who is the leader?

Is she using ostracism as a tool to encourage you to be better? Is your inability to penetrate the group not merit based? If not, what are the keys to entry, and do you really wish to pursue those keys?

Do your best

No approval scenario will overcome your best work. While you may always be an outsider, for as long as you are productive, you will have the singular benefit of self reliance and self worth. Being in the inner through good works has value, but cannot become your driving force.

The internal dialogue you have about your work, and overall philosophy driven by purpose will be much stronger over the long run than what work or social clique you penetrate.

GUILT

Riding the black horse to destroy your game plan is guilt. It is larger than shame, which comes from a deep internal feeling of being inadequate. Guilt strikes at your own feelings of how an action betrayed your own standards. The pain of guilt derives from a sense that you violated your own code and does not necessarily emanate from an outsider. However, like the other obstacles, guilt in the hands of someone we respect or must listen to in our life can be a powerful force to derail our developing world view.

There are few tasks that do not rely upon our expectations to achieve. Often we make a guess at how effective we will be as approach the challenge. Based upon our assessment of what it will take to accomplish the task, we assign a time frame, what attributes are needed, and how we will judge success. When the goal is concrete like completing a report or fixing an engine, the very linearity offers clear path to understanding if our efforts yielded the desired results.

This is more complex in dealing with others, especially those we seek to influence. The pathway here is wrought with turns and bumps. The person we hope to impact my not share our goals, reject our presence, or outright be defiant about our viewpoints. You may want to visit old friends on a trip, but your fiancé dislikes them, you go anyway. She makes it her mission to make you feel "guilty" for not spending time with her and not her family.

Voila'

Any sense of guilt come from the highly developed conscience that we all have developed through our upbringing. There are few men without one. It is a composite of your innate feelings of right and wrong that are survival mechanisms, and learned behaviors from observation. It is the active, present part of your being, it is unhidden and obvious. Under duress, and faced with frequent episodes that are guilt ridden, some revert to a life philosophy that are a being victimized by life, and validate their hostility to the world and others by blaming the victim of their actions, or, at least, refusing to accept responsibility for actions that harm others.

When we cross a barrier of expectations, our internal code signals a feeling of remorse and guilt, because we simply knew better than to act as we did. Rather than project our feeling of error upon others, we internalize the feelings, and allow ourselves to judge our actions against our own code, thus bringing on guilt. This reaction enables strong and narrow minded individuals to play on these feelings by imposing their code upon us. Thus, any action outside of the manipulators code, requires a forced compliance by others. It is this forced awareness that creates pain, as we attempt to reconcile one code with another. The more these views clash, the greater the pain, and inability to avoid guilt derived feelings.

While the present minded consciousness is coping with circumstances our unconscious mind is churning to balance the competing views. The unconscious is less obvious, subtle, harder to reach for most of us. It is a composite of feelings, experiences, and our future hopes. When we meditate, plan our future, set ideas into our mind, and even dream about our long term wishes, this collective power seems to guide us, and, at times, hold us back. It is our intuition, cognition, and sense of just, "knowing".

Those who want to manipulate our actions know that guilt is a motivator that causes significant anguish. It is so, because it pits our own values against ourselves, and forces us to face that we're not always capable of doing the right action. There is a personal commandment and we violate it, the pain we feel is guilt.

Feeling badly about an action is not going to stop your personal development,unless you allow it to become a recurring or defining script about yourself.

FIGHTING GUILT

What did you do?

Carefully review the action and assess the damage. Determine the size or proportion of the gaffe. Is this a violation of a core belief, a conflict of codes, or a minor

matter based upon a misunderstanding or lack of clarity in communication.
Who is Hurt?

Are you hearing from the person involved or from others? Who has the most to gain from you feeling guilty? Is this bout controlling your behavior, changing your code, or just imposing another persons will on you?

Getting it right

If you conclude that you did break your code, hurt someone, then a plan of action must be formulated to right the wrong. Feeling guilty can be a justified state if it prompts action and/or reforms your current code of ethics and operation.

Do not fear taking remedial action. It will free you and drive you towards your goals. But, do not delegate the action, you must do it yourself to become part of your revised method of operating in truth.

FEAR

The rider of the pale horse in Revelations was death, in our, analog, it is FEAR.

No emotion is more crippling to our dreams, indeed, just living day to day than this primordial fear. It comes from the same origin as anger, rises from the almond shaped organ inside our most primitive brain region, the amygdala. Just under the frontal portion of the temporal lobe.

We perceive or actually see danger, anticipate pain, sense threat, or are simply afraid, the hormones secrete, we prepare for a fight or to flee. Adrenalin pours into our bloodstream, blood flushes to our limbs, and our eyes focus upon the threat. Extraordinary, one might guess biologically, but it happens each day to some extent, and it can become chronic our fears become part of our very being.

The emotion evolved as the essential defense mechanism to preserve the species. How is it in your life? Is it a rare emotion that serves its original purpose. Or has it become, like it has for most men, a constant governor, or blockage to achieving a full, robust, and adventurous life. When fear rules a life, it creates problems not only for the realization of better philosophy, it stops progress mentally and physically. It can be so destructive as to mutate genes, clog arteries, and make men old before their time.

Living with and in fear is just not living.

All personal operating philosophies must assess risk and manage fear. But like the other horsemen, fear can be used by manipulators in our lives, to crush our game plans. The basic fears besides not having food, shelter, and good health, are well known to us all.

FEAR OF:

Failure

Almost everything of value that we hope to achieve can be stopped cold by this one. It is the most commonly mentioned fear among men surrounding any task. We are wired to accomplish things, succeed, and contribute. This fear looms large over every venture, it takes bold thinking, and risk to overcome it.

It is, however, proven by the life story of millions of men

that the road to success is paved with failures. You need only look at the biographies as diverse as Abraham Lincoln to Thomas Edison to observe that stamina, and self belief can overcome this fear and lead to success

Humiliation

This is a subset of shame. Our inner child craves support and familial love. The acts that can lead to humiliation, as we perceive it, often hold us back from richer life experiences. Romance, dating, richer social relationships all suffer if we give in to this fear. This fear often keeps people from pubic speaking, writing and the arts. So much is lost, if this humiliation forces a person away from their expression of love, or creativity.

Success

It may seem counterintuitive, but, winning and realizing specific goals can also threaten men. Even the most confident of men can hold a "knowing" inside them that too much success will harm them. Some of this feeling comes from a feeling of inadequacy and a deep belief that they do not deserve the success. It is, in its own way, a version of shame.

Loneliness

Some men are so afraid of being alone in life that they will accept any relationship to avoid it. This brand of insecurity comes from the belief that they are not worthy of being with others and they will act forcefully to foster relationships. This fear can drive dependency, and force a man towards others, without much thought or space between couplings. At its most extreme, it can reverse itself, where a man is so exhausted by seeking companions that he finally opts for seclusion.

Rejection

This is less about failing than it is about going for something to be shunned by the players in the game. It is the fear of not being accepted, even if you are able to compete and comport yourself admirably. Again this a group dynamic influencing our choices. You may be able to play rugby, follow Texas Hold'em, dance a tango, but fear of rejection by the others can end your pursuit.

It is a fear that addresses failure to engage in recreation to more serious pursuits. Where there is a group or single influencer who can rebuff your efforts, rejection can overcome your training, instincts to engage, and,even, your ultimate contribution.

Intimacy

After too many turn downs, failed relationships, or a cold family upbringing, any man can fear offering himself to intimacy. The very thought of crossing a barrier from merrily being together to commitment that requires a deeper bond can be frightening.

Reaching for intimacy can suggest failure, rejection, and even loneliness is not achieved. It is rarely physical intimacy that is the greatest fear, although that can exist. It is the bold reality of being engaged with a person and their inner self, almost unspeakable place that unifies two people, two souls.

The fear can easily overtake a man who has been manipulated by women, and has never felt loved without condition.

Loss of Control

This fear crosses into many barriers of the psyche. Whether it is fear of falling in love, missing real threats, being vulnerable to others, or losing yourself in the lives of others and failing to live the life you want, control is required.

If a man sees that this control mechanism is tenuous, everything can be lost. It is as frightening as jumping out of a plane, and lasts much, much longer.

OVERCOMING FEARS

There are libraries of texts on conquering fears like those mentioned and others from phobias to threats that are solely imagined in distorted minds. For most of us, of relatively sound mind, with conscience and unconscious influences, fears are real, not just part of our imagination. There are fears that are un warranted, that require special help to overcome from fear of spiders to claustrophobia. But, the fears that can destroy our philosophy of life can be faced straight on and conquered. They become a problem when we let others use them as weapons against us.

THE HORSEMEN CAN BE DEFEATED

The defeat of our horsemen delivering dissonance to our game plans is up to each of us.

It is about our certainty that our quest to develop a game plan, based upon a philosophy of life and a code of operation, is essential to our development. If we allow manipulators to employ shame, approval, guilt and fear to alter our path we have only ourselves to blame.

The path you are on is righteous, if you believe in it. There is no horseman that can trample you, once you have resolved to live your life, on your path, and no one elses.

WHAT ARE YOU PREPARED TO DO?

Who are your manipulators?

Can you identify situations, where the horsemen enter your life?

Are you afraid of fighting these forces? If so why are you afraid?

Keep an accounting of when you feel manipulated, and plot how you get over it.

CHAPTER V

The Big Three; Think, Say, Consume

"You must act as though you are already there. Destroy the old you and transform."

Neville Goddard

As you carry yourself daily is how you will be judged. All viable personal operating philosophies depend upon action, not only thought and dutiful consideration. It may seem a surface judgement but it is the essential beginning of that transformation you are seeking. The first steps of the actual change in the way you live our life takes place internally and reveals itself externally, in actions, speech and appearance.

The significant sea change starts with your thinking about who want to become. There is not a single self help guru who has not based their entire program on,"changing your thinking; create a plan ; and act". While this has merit, it fails if what you are thinking is based upon prior images of who you are, or a vision of the past, shrouded by a limited game plan. Neville Goddard, who claimed to have learned his theories from the mystic, Abdullah, the Ethiopian, had a simple, yet, challenging message: to immediately begin to think like, talk like; and consume like the man you want to be. Then, over time, almost imperceptibly you begin to transform into the life and person you imagine.

Imagination is not about fantasy trips. We all have those. Winning the SuperBowl, a grand slam in tennis, or playing at Carnegie Hall. No, this imagining what you can achieve based upon your attributes, intellect, and, of course, your desire and will. But, you must see an image of yourself; how you look, speak, your posture, dress, and general comportment. If you imagine a corporate office and a boardroom, then you must also imagine that you cannot continue to speak with expletives in each sentence. F..k cannot be your favorite modifier. If you slump from place to place, or wear the same pants each day, you are projecting an image that is not the person you want to be. If you eat 3,000 calories a day of fast food, you will grow thick and age poorly.

If you set an image of the man you want to become, and then act upon it, you will realize the game plan of your life. It takes courage, and is done in increments, one act, one thought at a time, a sentence that has heart and meaning, a posture of a man who owns his destiny and is attentive to his life.

WHAT YOU THINK

Take a journey inside your active mind. Are you able to focus on a single task? Do you find that your thoughts are clustered and, at times, you obsess upon trivial matters?

Are you dwelling on the past or worrying about future prospects?

There is enough science to conclude that we do not multi task effectively. The brain is more powerful focused on a single matter, or series of actions. Being about the moment in front of you, whether it is a phone call, a text, or a conversation, clears the mind for action and puts all your cognitive powers into play. Daydreaming, distracted thinking all enter our consciousness, when we are bored, disinterested or are compelled by the next series of events. But, clarity comes from focus, and realizing when a meeting, talk, or call has lost our attention. Every thought event has a horizon, that differs depending upon circumstances, when you reach the attention horizon, any time you are spending is wasted and often counterproductive.

As you assess your daily thinking chart these factors, you may be surprised how much time is for perfunctory matters and how little cognitive time is spent on acting upon creating the life you want. To put it bluntly:

How much time in this life are you spending each day on creating the life you want ?

Thinking About:

    Commute; Shopping
    Body preparation and dressing
    Food Choices
    Relationships
    Family Issues
    Finances
    Recreation choices

WORK

The Game Plan for Change

For most men work commands the largest percentage of daily thought, and there is little brain time left for most other thoughts. Obviously, unless time is dedicated to the game plan it cannot happen. You cannot dream it, will it, or luck into it. Some portion of your thinking must be about who you want to become, what you need to do to get there, and what you need to put aside or destroy to open time for pursuit of your philosophy.

Creating the Time

It is a challenge to get this new personal operating philosophy into your life. Some of it is organic, you have a code to follow, a guiding philosophy, and now you need to take small actions to achieve more of the game plan. Here are some insights:

Write out each week two to three steps that are important to you. Keep them on your list until you get them done. Rarely will you accomplish them all in a week. It may take a month or year, who cares, any step makes a difference. They can be uncomplicated like buying a new razor to avoid razor bumps; or start buying a new pair of shoes; or taking up Aikido. But, each should suggest the man you want to become. There can also be complexity learn a language, start painting, buy a shotgun, spend time with your daughter.

Some guys like a master list that defines the totality of the transformation, a bucket list of change. They check each off, to force themselves to review what steps they are taking to get on a game plan. It does not matter if you stay with the plan or check off all the items. What does matter is that you are taking action towards a new game plan that you have created.

And by acting, you may find a need to change the plan, adapt, and regroup. This is the process, of course. You will develop through this introspective drill a "knowing" about whether this chosen path has heart or not. If it has heart you will stay with it, if not, you will chose another path. You have lost nothing taking one path, and, rejecting it. There is no judgment to be made between men.

Three Minute Meditation

Cleansing the mind offers real value as you create a game plan for your life. Some suggest long term meditation or the "practice" as it is called. There is no debate that all forms of meditation whether zen based or included in active yoga exercises provide a calming benefit over time.

But, not all men find this clear mind experience to fit their day. There is so much to develop as the new philosophy matures that this three minute pause may be idela for men at work.

It requires nothing but three minutes, to sit alone, anywhere, in your car, truck, or office to get quiet, breathe deeply, and let all thoughts go. The idea is to release yourself from the world for three minutes. It may seem easy, but it requires a commitment to do it, when you can do it without interruption.

Do not do it when you re agitated or angry. It is not a long enough time to process those feelings. It is best utilized when you are at ease, slightly overwhelmed or just can feel your mind struggling with far too many thoughts.

6 Breaths of Freedom

There are any number of transitions in our days. Getting into the car, walking into the office, visiting with the boss, preparing for the workout, returning home from work, the evening rituals. We often go from event to event, automatically, never considering what the next event will require of us. Sometimes, we transfer energy, positive and negative, from one event to the other, even though, they are not, remotely connected.

You have witnessed how this lack of pausing and collecting energy and approaches can railroad the next event. You have not decompressed from a contentious staff meeting and you immediately throw yourself into a phone call with your wife; you drove through the rush hour and immediately enter the house to be overwhelmed by the family; you attempt a discussion about the use of the car by your son, just as you received a text from your boss.

Take a six breath pause.

It will give you a moment to review the next event. You will be forced to marshal your thoughts and emotions to prepare for the next moment. Athletes take a few moments, before the serve, at the gate on a ski run, get set before a play on the field, or before a sprint race. It is a way to get ready, set yourself, with six deep inhales.

You find that it gives you a small respite and freedom, between things. These pauses center us, and give us renewed power to act and observe.

What You Say

The best representation of what a man is really becoming is exhibited in his language. It is the window into your mind and reveals quickly what you think of yourself and the impact you seek to have upon others. While, it may seem that good deal of thought goes into our speech, when you observe yourself, you notice how much is automatic, that rarely thinks through what we are saying or its impact on others. In fact, our speech can fall into obvious patterns that are not about growth or transformation, but just day to day communication.

Often our patterns are derived from the cultural value we place on the communication. We choose vocabulary, tonality, use of humor and sarcasm, and deference based upon our perception of others. You will talk differently to your siblings, parents, children, friends and perceived influencers, like your fellow workers.

Your growth is as much about how you perceive your speech as, how you are received by others. It is not just what you say, but when do you speak, the use of words to be expressive, your pacing, volume and purpose. What comes out of your mouth is a critical in achieving your game plan as any other aspect of your presentation.

There is no one who is successful in their field who has not adopted a mode of expression, speech, that fits their life plan. An NFL coach and a psychiatrist have different patterns; the lawyer uses the language differently than a fighter pilot; your barber different than your internist. This does not mean that all do not meet certain norms of acceptable speech, or that a cab driver might not speak like a professor. But, usually, people adopt the patterns, pace, and vocabulary of that they wish to become.

Unfortunately, if you walk into any casual setting, where men congregate, like a bar or restaurant or ball game, you will hear speech patterns that once were prevalent in lower socio-economic neighborhoods or among un educated thugs. These patterns,while used in these casual places do seep into day to day speech and lower the quality of communication between men.

Often these sentences are sprinkled with expletives as modifiers and for emphasis.

"I can't believe she fuckin said that to him, who the fuck does she think she is anyway"

"That motherfucker has no business callin the shots, anyway, who the fuck does he think he is, what the fuck does he know"

"He is such a cocksucker, do you think he has any idea what the fuck he is doing that motherfucker"

Or

"How can that shithead, tell me what to do, he has shit for brains"

It can be difficult to cull the expletives from speech in less casual settings. The result is obvious. The man who does not use the curse words to get attention, make a point or be regarded as a peer will be closer to a code that serves him well over the long term. People are often startled and in awe of someone who reserves the expletive for rare use.

One deep thinker and guide, Deepak Chopra had some insight on speaking that fits our transformational quest. He asks, when you speak does it meet these criteria:

Is it necessary?

Is it helpful ?

Is it kind?

Is it critical? Hurtful?

Is it to blow off steam?

Is it from anger?

Is it to make fun or humor?

And then, he urges whether to speak or not, or listen. Also, for how long?

While this may seem an obvious checklist, few of us go through any pre- talk list at all. We often blurt out whatever comes to mind, and have to compensate after the fact. How many utterances were at the expense of another ? How many times did you want the words back in an argument or confrontation? It is difficult to pre- think, have the presence to always speak on the right topic, with precisely the proper tone and inflection, and vocabulary. It is unrealistic to be that perfect to be that fully evolved intellectually. Still, Dr. Chopra knows that attention here can bring significant gains for a man in search of a higher calling.

Our vocabulary is a soundtrack of our thoughts. It changes based upon setting, circumstance and receptors. But there must be a constant foundation for speech that defines and elevates us and suggests our essential selves. You cannot effectively monitor all of your speech mannerisms, but there are patterns you can be aware of, and just the awareness will improve your communication skills:

Speech patterns

Why am I speaking?

Declare presence
Give direction or guidance
Make a point
Embrace the speaker, and being supportive
Achieving a specific result
Small talk- for inclusion
Blow off steam
Appear clever/humorous/sarcasm
Praise/ Critique
Bonding
Change viewpoint/ be supportive of view
To Argue
Sooth emotions/ assist in coping

Should I speak

Is this the right time?
What am I adding/subtracting
Is silence better?
Am I listening enough?
Duration of my response?

Vocabulary

Have I adjusted by words to fit the situation and the group?

Can I maintain a non – expletive pattern ?

Have I improved my word selection and use of a broader word selection?

Is it clear my speech is improving and growing?

What comes out of your mouth is a clear indicator of who you are and who you want to become. You cannot think you are growing and finding a new path, unless you begin to use the language patterns of who you want to become. Fortunately, this process of reforming your speech requires nothing more than the will to change.

WHAT YOU CONSUME

Changing your mindset, being mindful of your speech, are easy matters when compared to asking a man to be mindful of what he puts into his mouth. It is beyond a personal matter, men will offer argument and a litany of reasons, why what they put into their "piehole" has no impact on their philosophy,or game plan for life. Consumption of ideas, thoughts, and purpose are fine, but consumption is,somehow, sacrosanct.

It is certainly true that you can realize dreams, achieve a superior lifestyle and eat poorly, drink too much, and develop addictions from overindulgence and poor consumptive habits. But, there is no reason to not explore your awareness of what you consume, and how it can hamper your own quality of life.

Eat to Live or Live to Eat

Two views of food where either viewpoint can meet the basic requirement of fueling activity and survival. An argument can be made that both when reviewed with care can provide the nutrients required to offer essential fats, proteins, and carbohydrates to live well.

The average adult male needs 2000-2500 calories at the most robust diet level. Men that take in less than 2000 calories are usually stronger, flexible, and more alert than those that consume more, especially if the intake is more carb and lean protein based, with less fats. While exercise and movement certainly plays a role, quality of life studies show that diet matters 70 per cent, and exercise and genetics the rest. You can overcome bad genes, and create amazing cardiovascular fitness, but you cannot overcome, French fries, ribs, cake, waffles, burritos, all in the same day.

What you put into your mouth would profit from some criteria, besides caloric density. A working plan might include an awareness of what you are eating nutritionally; its caloric load; nutrient contribution; and how your system adapts to it. An extra soda, a 300 calorie a day bag of chips, can add significant weight to even a strenuous exercising or active lifestyle man.

If you are driven by your palate and taste, just be aware of the load you consume. You can satisfy taste needs and enjoy your diet, with smart selection and some pre – planning. If you can keep any given day under 2500 calories, you have a shot at maintaining a reasonable weight that will not block your long term game plan. After all, once you do the hard work of reviewing your goals and philosophy, you do not want your weight or physical condition to get in your way.

Habit Driven and Emotional Eating

So much of our eating is habit driven. The morning coffee and cake, the afternoon lunch with colleagues, the required family dinner. These events tie us to others and are about socialization. As you would expect, the opportunity to be comfortable, enjoy others, increases our caloric intake. Sometimes we are taking seconds and eating our way through the event, because the food is providing us comfort, and calming us, as the occasion may have its own hidden stressors.

Everyone overeats at traditional dinners, like Thanksgiving, as much due to coping with the family and the stress, as because the food is plentiful. Often food fills holes within us, and offers temporary relief from the demands of a crowded life. It is only a problem when you cannot see that the extra beers, the run to the refrigerator is a way to deal with issues without touching them. You know, the food will not solve the problem, fill an emotional hole or move you forward towards a solution.

Here as in our other discussions awareness is the most reliable tool to control our habits and emotions. Just a moment, a nano moment, to ask why you are about to open that fridge door, pull that lever at the canteen machine, or pop open another beer, can give you the presence of mind to reject the item, or at least, limit your consumption.

Consuming for habit alone or to fill an emotional hole is a poor substitute for being conscious of what you are doing to fuel your brain and body. You have more at stake now as you construct this game plan for your life.

The Food Journal

If you really want to get alert to what you are consuming, take a few weeks and keep a food journal. It does not need to be fancy or contrived. No need to count calories or give points for food sources. This is not a Weight Watchers or Richard Simmons exercise. You can find enough weight loss programs, if you decide you need them. This is the raw facts of your food intake, then you can assess it.

Write down, somewhere for two weeks, everything you eat or drink. Everything.

Most men are so unconscious when they eat, that this simple journal immediately turns them in a more rational direction. After you jot this down, think if you would have the guts to show it to your children, your buddies on your team, or worse, your doctor. If it shames you into a new awareness it will have done its job. And, if it is reasonable and overall healthy, it should offer some insights into how you can improve your intake.

You would be hard put to find a man who would show you his food journal. What we put in our mouths is a secret as what we really do in our bedrooms. And less discussed. If you have the inclination, suggest to your few best friends that you keep a journal for two weeks and then compare them, and vow to improve your intake accordingly.

BONUS TRAITS for YOUR PERSONAL OPERATING PHILOSOPHY

The Strenuous Life

You do not have to commit to a strenuous life to construct POP that works for you. This is your transformation and not that anyone else should impose. A strenuous life is a life that includes some imposed actual, not figurative sweat, some real heavy lifting or weight bearing exercise and a commitment to make it an integral part of this new, emerging life path. What we have observed and seen through the study of the lives of men who have made such a commitment is this; they do not always live longer, avoid the bumps, holes and turns in the path of life, they just seem to be able to enjoy it all more.

And it is not determined by work either. Some few of us still have agrarian lives that require daily activity of farming, plowing, tending fields. And few of us who are blessed with the skills of craftsmen or devoted our lives to public service in firehouses or in police cruisers. These men lead strenuous lives by the nature of their vocations, intellects and skills. For the rest of us, who sit more than we move, activity that is hard and tough is of value.

Men as diverse as Mr. America and Hercules fame, Steve Reeves, power walked up mountains his entire life; philosopher Friedrich Nietzsche, was a walker, who developed his themes trekking through Swiss mountain tops, some men, ran marathons into his 80's, starting at 76. Their desire was to be active, and fight back against age and decay.

As America began recruiting for WWI, the draft found men sickly, and pigeon chested. They had no stamina, and possessed limbs that were weak and devoid of powerful muscles. They were lean, but weak. Now one hundred years later, the United States Army has had to lower their recruitment standards because men are too fat, with enlarged waistlines, and no stamina. These unfit recruits suffer from chronic disease, obesity, poor nutrition, and an inability to focus upon tasks.

There is a mythology afoot, that America has fitter men, who eat well, sweat each day, and test their mettle. Sadly, only a small population is committed to a sound body as well as a resourceful outlook and a sound mind. Your commitment to a POP, can include this strenuous life with little real effort or time.

What we know about the inclusion of this in your game plan is that it can transform your body, your internal organs, and will actually change your genetic makeup. This type of exercise can bring about morphogenetic benefits. From your blood health to your brain function and focus, this life choice can bring enormous bonus benefits to your game plan for life.

Base Plan

Three hours a week of cardiovascular work- any form, but with this array of options

Five minute warm up
Talking speed for 20 minutes
Five minute warm down

Or

Five minute warm up

20 minutes at tempo, level of exertion at 6-7 on (1-10 scale)
Five minute warm down

Or

Five minute warm up
Ten minutes at 6-7
Ten minutes at 7
Five minute warm down

Or

Five minute arm up
One minute at 7-9 (intervals)
One minute at 5-6
One minute 7-9 (repeat cycle for twenty minutes)
Warm down

This mix of slower effort and then interval work, will offer variety for the week. Pick an activity you like or will stay with, from running, to fast walking, to gym gear.

And then lift weights or do push ups and sit ups, with planks everyday.

This provides the basis for a strenuous lifestyle. From this you can launch yourself at more epic goals, whether racing or pick up games with friends. If you integrate the effort into you week, you will see immediate benefits. Overtime, it will become a positive habit that will drive you to do more and expand your experiences. As long as you have the ability to sweat it out, there is no reason to deny yourself, these significant benefits.

You will be more alert, solve problems faster, have good

brain health, improve your blood work and widen your arteries. And you will begin to feel transformed from within.

HARDINESS

Being hard is not just a function of being fit, eating better. It is an attitude possessed by men with bold, world views and powerful philosophies of life. It is the most important survival quality. It is a companion of our outlook, it is a subset of how we see the world and how we carry ourselves in it. Hardy people survive. Hardy people are not unnerved by even the most unsettling aspects of life. This quality is already expanding inside you as you have taken steps to review your life and how you can change it for the better.

Here is what is happening to you as you pursue your personal operating philosophy.

You are:

Tougher towards changing elements in your life, less bothered

Slower to anger

Have a series of do's and don'ts based upon a life code

Resistant to manipulation based upon emotions

In control of a conscious,uncluttered mind

Speak thoughtfully and with purpose

Aware of what you consume, nutritionally and from the culture at large

Seek to be well and as healthy as possible to assist in reaching goals

When life comes at you, you can respond with authority, and you do not collapse in fear. Even if you sustain an emotional hit or obstacle, you are ready to plot a new strategy, adapt, and move forward. While, you cannot see the future, you have coping mechanisms to handle any eventuality. People turn to you for direction and leadership in crisis. You know there will be drama, disasters, and, even, surprises, but you not curse them, you embrace the problems because you know you can find answers.

Hardiness is a complex of traits that you are owning. They emanate from a deep belief system that surrounds some core principles.

"Everything is self limiting. All things have a cycle, a beginning, a middle and an end. There is an impermanent nature to everything, nothing is permanent, everything shifts over time. Whatever happens is within my power to deal with it, as I can link one moment to another and stay focused on what each requires of me. I am committed to what is happening now, I have goals, and I respect the lessons of the past, but my only real impact is now. I am prepared to let go, be unattached to outcomes, and believe that I am not ever alone as I seek to find my best self"

And that is what being hardy is all about

WHAT WILL YOU DO ?

Develop a 30 day plan to be more active.

Keep a food diary to see what you are eating. Eat more for life than taste, or to fill an emotional hole.

Try to say as little as possible once a week, and assess the impact of your silence.

Can you think optimistically for a full day, with no negative thoughts?

CHAPTER VI

What Do You Believe In? Faith

"All the Gods, all the heavens, all the hells,
are within you ."

Joseph Campbell

It is difficult to find a man who does not have faith in something. It may even be the fundamentals of physics or the rise and fall of the sun and the moon. There is a natural instinct to believe that some force either of nature or man, that we cannot control exists. For some men it is a backdrop to their philosophy for others faith is an essential driving force in life. Others live their lives with no nod to anything that might exist besides themselves, they are driven by the vagaries of the day to day and either just do not believe in anything beyond what they can measure, or have rejected faith as a foolish concept.

Joseph Campbell, studied all religions and developed a theory of the founding mythologies of faith based philosophies, that we commonly call religions. They all have a God, or supreme being. They have a goal or purpose for believers. Often they provide a view of an afterlife and a way believers practice the faith. There also is usually a tradition and rule book, that outlines the way for believers, contained in a text like a Bible, Torah, or Koran. These common elements serve to guide a man through his life, and offer insights into how to live a life of faith and righteousness.

Campbell also found that ancient faiths had a founding mythology that often found man as battling forces external and internal to find their true self, that propelled man on a journey to fight forces on a heroic journey to self realization. It is, of course, the fundamental plot of anything, man has goals, fights forces in his way, finds the path and triumphs. This is the stuff of Hollywood, where conflict and challenge is resolved by the time the credits roll in the theater.

It is rarely as linear in reality. Our hero struggle has turns and holes in the road, and, at times, we are so exhausted by the process, we want to pull over. But, depending upon your personal operating philosophy, and your hardiness, you go on. For some men this thing called faith makes the journey less arduous. The saying that a man may be an atheist before the shooting starts, but everyone is praying once the battle begins is not lost upon generations of veterans. Still, others, emerge from such carnage faithless, convinced that no God would allow the events of war, murder, or mayhem to ever occur.

To be sure you do not have to have faith, or religion to develop a rational and purposeful Manosophy. The development of values that guide you, and how you conduct yourself towards others, requires no God, rule book, or congregation. However, billions of men have a faith, to some measure, that serves to offer them direction, solace, and an extra code of conduct that layers onto their philosophy or is, in fact, its foundation.

What are some of these faiths and how might they factor into the construction of your own worldview.

Abrahamic Faith

Judaism, Christianity, and Islam all have their roots in the story of Abraham. The concept of a single God emerges, and the progeny of Abraham generates the line of descendants that emerge over time into the main religious figures of each faith, including Moses and Aaron, Christ and the prophet Mohammed.

Christianity

There are about 2.2 billion Christians. They believe in a God, who is a trinity of the Father, the Son (Jesus), and Holy Spirit. Jesus is the son of God and is the Messiah. Man is separated from God by sin, and salvation comes through a combination of faith in Jesus, and living a life of good works. And a believer can have everlasting life through a total commitment to Christ. The guiding text is the New testament, and secondarily the Old Testament. There is a strong belief in redemption and the emergence of a new world after Christ returns to earth in the "second coming", the end of a period of Revelation.

Judaism

There are only 14 million Jews in the world. While the original foundational faith of Abraham, lack of conversion, low birth rate, and mass extermination has reduced Jewish followers to less than 0.2 % of the world's believers. There is a single God, Yahweh or Jehovah. The way of life is defined in the Ten Commandments, the Torah (Bible), and the Talmud, that interprets the Jewish life. There is a "world to come" that is realized upon the coming of a Messiah. To Jews, Jesus was not the Messiah referenced in their texts. But, the emphasis on heaven and hell is muted, as believers are expected to live good lives on earth, and "repair the world". Boys are circumcised at birth, and come of age at 13. There are dietary restrictions on shellfish, pork, the mix of foods, commonly referred to as Kosher rules.

Islam

This is the most recent of the Abrahamic faiths, founded in 622 CE, by the Prophet Mohammed. It has over 1.6 billion adherents. Allah is the one God, that requires submission to faith in him and adherence to practices that will provide a pathway to heaven, or Paradise, after death. The Qur'an establishes the practices and story of Islam. It is based upon Five Pillars ; Faith, Prayer, Alms, Pilgrimage, and Fasting. There are dietary rituals, prohibiting eating pork and drinking alcohol. Boys are also circumcised as a birthing ritual. It is the fastest growing major religion and its faith tenets are held by men across a broad spectrum from orthodoxy to moderate, more assimilated faith versions.

A note on the intensity of faith.

While each faith has believers who will self –identify, the intensity of their belief from orthodoxy to more moderate forms of observance is vast. Often some bundle of beliefs will be considered essential to be of a faith, and for some, just being born into the faith is enough to create a bond of some measure. Usually the essential bond is the belief in the God of the faith, the central theme that surrounds that story, and some manner of selected practice. Thus, while church going, or attendance at a Mosque satisfies billions of believers, it may not be part of the belief system of any given Muslim or Christian. The range of practice is obviously a unique and personal matter, that in many ways defines a person, and certainly can offers insights into their personal operating philosophy, if it is faith based at all.

Buddhism

A belief system founded by Siddhartha Gautama, the Buddha, around 520 BC. It has 500 million followers. Has many deities, that are revered for differing attributes. But, the major theme is constant. There is a cycle of birth and rebirth, and the goal is to attain enlightenment or nirvana. The path to this is through the living of a righteous life. Buddha taught that there is suffering in life, but that it can be lessened and relieved by following certain truths of right action, speech, three, and four. The afterlife is the realization of the end of suffering, in nirvana. Buddhists practice, meditation, yoga, mindfulness, and development of the inner spirit. It is a diverse faith, that has many sects, influences, god like figures. It is often seen by western believers as less a faith than a practice to clear your mind, and set a path of tolerance, kindness, right action, and peacefulness.

Hinduism

Over a billion people follow this very ancient faith that dates back to over 1500 BCE. While it has supreme being, or reality, the Brahman, there are many gods and goddesses as part of the worship process. It also has a belief in reincarnation, or rebirth, that each life yields to another as a being moves towards enlightenment. Each person has a purpose or dharma, and journeys to attempt to explore and engage that purpose,in the hope that it will lead to a more enlightened life. Hindus will also employ meditation, yoga, prayer to many gods, and pilgrimage to holy cities as a practice of their faith.

Deism

Is by and large a lost faith. But, it had real importance to the 18th century framers of our constitution. It was rooted in the philosophy of the Enlightenment, where reason and belief in what was observable was in vogue. Tom Paine and Tom Jefferson, in the pre-scientific age, saw this as a valid description of how the universe came to be. They saw a God, who was the creator, but who then left the world and its occupants to their own devices. It is the "clockmaker" view of creation and the aftermath. In its own way, it encouraged freedom of thought, liberty, and everything based upon what they called, an "Age of Reason". There were no rituals, although these 18th century philosophes did, at times get caught in prayer.

Mormon

Another more modern faith, founded in 1830, by New Yorker, Joseph Smith, and with a flock of over 12.5 million. It is another fast growing faith in the world. It came to Smith in a revelation from an angel, Moroni, and separates the father (God) from Jesus and the Holy Ghost. They believe in good works, conversion, after death baptism, and faith in Christ. Mormons believe in a path to heaven, and hell for non believers. They have the Book of Mormon, once inscribed upon gold plates, long lost. They also have strict practices that include prohibition of alcohol,caffeine, eternal marriage and the wearing of garments. They experienced a period of persecution, that was eventually offset by the establishment of their settlement near the Great Salt Lake and the solidification of the Church of the Later Day Saints under the temporal and secular leadership of Brigham Young.

Other Belief Systems

There are, of course, many other beliefs that have roots in the main faiths, or derive their faith from specific founders, and their interpretation of the way the world was created, who rules it, and what practices are required to move towards a well lived life, that is a balance of devotion to God's wishes, or the development of inner wisdom that offers a pathway to heaven, another existence, or a return to dust.

And while there are billions who self –identify with some faith, there a billion others who have no attachment to any affiliation. Are they less imbued with a guiding philosophy or game plan? Whether there is a designation, that billion also has faith in something, even if it is, in their certainty, that there is no creator, guiding force or principle that must be following to achieve a fulfilling life.

Each faith has elements that speak to the same yearning to define a purpose that fulfills the place of man in this world, and prepares him for whatever is next. For Confucians, it is honesty and loyalty, and acting properly in society. For Jehovah's Witnesses, it is seeking salvation through Christ, and only 144,000 getting to heaven, the rest having an eternity on earth, while everyone else vanishes to nothingness. To Ron Hubbard's Scientologists, great things can be accomplished as you rid your reactive mind of "engrams" and become "clear" through certain mental practices and training. For Sikhism, the practice is to balance work, worship, and giving, believing in one God, or one Supreme Reality, Onkar.

Tao has 20 million followers, who follow the teachings of Lao-Tzu, from 550 BC, that encourage a "way" of life that is based upon non- attachment, end of struggle, and the highly regarded and well known phrase, "go with the flow". And even the most recent faith, Rastafarianism, founded by civil rights leader, Marcus Garvey in Jamaica in 1920's, has its tenets that are universal. God is Jah, who appeared in human form as Jesus. Redemption is within each man, and salvation comes with being free. For Garvey this required a return to Africa. Practices include a restricted diet, adoption of many ancient Hebrew traditions, and the use of marijuana for religious and medical healing.

You can probably find some faith that reflect your own world view, but,perhaps, not all the tenets will be appealing. This is, of course, what makes for an act of faith. It requires belief in the entirety of the religion to be totally committed. Across this spectrum from orthodoxy to reformation, aspects of a faith fall off. You may believe that Jesus was the son of God, and that if you believe in him you will have an everlasting life. But you may never step foot in a church. As a Jew, you may go to temple on the High Holy days of Rosh Hashanah and Yom Kippur, and never again throughout the year. You may pray privately and follow the Qur'an, but not follow all the other requirements of Islam. Each faith, however, has its lines in the sand.

The fundamental requirement is the faith in the founding story or myth. For the Abrahamic faiths it is a faith that is one God, who has offered a prescription for life and a sense of results that come with such a life. But, even here the stories differ, on who is most blessed, is there a Messiah, has he come or not, who is chosen, is heaven gotten through Christ or the Prophet's view of Allah, and on and on. It is about accepting some faith or not. A path, if you will to spiritual fulfillment and solace when needed.

Again that spectrum of faith is vast. One the one pole are those who say, "everything for a reason, and God has a plan" to "I believe in something bigger than me, but, whatever that is, is also inside of me and I can access it.." Don Juan said to Carlos Castaneda, find a path with heart and follow it, all you need to learn about yourself is there, or if not simply chose another path. To Don Juan there was no judgment to be made, no penalty. The penalty was to your soul, if you followed a heartless path that turned your heart to stone and dissolved your spirit and shriveled your soul.

Joseph Campbell following that logic with some humor,

"As you proceed through life, following your own path, birds will shit on you. Don't bother to brush it off. Getting a comedic view of your situation gives you spiritual distance. Having a sense of humor saves you."

But, it is hard to be light in spirit, and un attached as you approach the daily issues of your life. Some men find it helps to have faith in something, that becomes a best friend and confidant as you deal with your challenges. Faith can help you gain perspective, throw off attacks, and,most critically, encourage you to get back up and never give in to fatigue, doubt, fears or perceived defeats.

Most men find the eternal debate over whether there is a God, a perplexing and theoretical/scientific sidebar to life. It is not a topic often engaged by men in groups, ballfields, or at work. Even, in more reflective time, the essential element of faith is rarely examined. It is because,the arguments are not soluble through pure reason or from observation. There is a leap required, and it is celestial in proportion.

Current thinking is that this universe is 13.8 billion years old. A mass of unimaginable weight was reduced to a single particle mass. Then, somehow the physics of this mass, created an explosion, that sent everything we now know as the universe spewing outward. This begat gases, elements, solid masses, stars, planets, you know the rest. And today special earth based telescopes can see light from 12.8 billion year ago. And even, if you acknowledge all of that, what we cannot see in dark energy, and dark matter is greater than what we can observe.

And some experts claim that if set of circumstances can, by laws of astrophysics,posit this universe, is it likely there may be others, the multi- verse concept. Then, does each universe have its own God, its own creator, or is the one God of Abraham, the God of all these forces? The questions get broader, and more complex if you are looking for science or logic to get you to an explanation. Did a God create the Bing Bang, if not an entity, then a comic force that has no consciousness? Was the God not only a creator, but a God with an awareness of man, his foibles and his destiny on this earth?

You can create any founding myth you wish, but, anyone of them will require a reckoning with faith. Reason and observation take you only so far, and cannot construct a robust system, without the special ingredient of "I believe". You could agree that the universe is one and only, and that there was a single moment when it all began, but the question remains whether or not a force ignited it- and is that force knowing; omnipresent; or distant. Caring and directive or non existent to fit your own world view. Can you blend your element of faith into your personal operating philosophy or does it underpin it?

The Operative Questions for Assessment of Faith in your POP
GOD
Do you believe in God?
Is this a knowing God, who watches over you and offers direction?

Does this God have a pre-ordained path for you to follow?
Does this God create your life and universe, but leaves to find your way
Is God inside of you, and you but need to reveal his presence through your actions?

Relationship to GOD
Am I to follow his teachings to achieve good life?
What is my path to salvation or redemption?
Am I born into sin ?
Am I born good ?
What is state of Spirit and Soul?

Practices
What must I do to have this faith
What are my daily rituals
Long term observances, holidays, pilgrimages
Rites of passage, boy to man rites,
Dietary restrictions, use of drugs
Meditation, yoga ?
Where does it all lead
Is there life after death
What is heaven and hell concept
Is there rebirth
Is reincarnation in this world or others
Is my only life this,life and how do I conduct myself with faith

TEXTS
What are the existing guidance books
Bible and New Testament
Quran
Book of Mormon

The Four Fold Path (Buddhism)
Scientology
The Tao (Lao Tzu)
Zen
Shambhala

THE EFFORT TO UNDERSTAND FAITH

Any man can have a Manosophy, without traditional or any faith based concepts. Yet, without faith, there will always be a spiritual, if un-affiliated reference point. From our very beginnings there was an instinct, perhaps, a drive to connect ourselves with something that is beyond ourselves. All of us knowing that there is a connection between men that is cosmic that unites us on this planet as men who are about good deeds, accomplishment, progress, and capable of great teaching, fatherhood, and love.

What unites us are these genetic traits to protect and provide and defend at all costs, including the loss of our own lives. Sacrifice, devotion and caring, define all men. But only those of us blessed to be in a free society have the opportunity to rise above basic needs and contemplate how powerful,we can be. This process of refection is what creates a unified word view, and the role faith can play in our will to be transformed into the best we can become.

This notion that men are born unredeemed or flawed, is part of many faiths. It drives men to explore their inner being and through faith achieve a connection to higher values. You can chose such a faith or not, there are enough frightening examples of the horrors men can bring to the world, including men, committed to a faith, distorted though it may have been proven to be by events.

It takes some time, effort, and no small part of courage to confront these issues. But, like our other challenges, getting in touch with your faith, and the requirements of practicing it will only further craft your emerging philosophy and empower your gameplan.

WHAT ARE YOU PREPARED TO DO?

Examine your faith. Are you traditionally religious? Do you feel spiritual?

Discuss your faith with pastor or loved ones, what impact does it have on your lifestyle?

If you had no faith, what would steer you spiritually?

Can you live with your beliefs and to what extent?

CHAPTER VII

Sex: The Gordian Knot

"There are several knots all tightly entangled, whoever unravels them will rule all of Asia"

A Phrygian Soothsayer

Any philosophy of any man must consider the role sex plays in life. It is a topic that brings argument, as men, have widely divergent views of what role it should play, where sex leads, and its place in proportion to other pursuits. It is in many ways man's Gordian Knot, an impossible tangle of emotions, that knot up our minds and torment our bodies; or, release our pain, cares, and offer comfort, solace and pleasure.

A peasant named Gordias came to an ancient town, Phrygia, and had his oxen cart lashed to a post, by the King's son, Midas. The knot remained for many years, and grew tougher to unravel. Alexander the Great entered around 400 BCE, and was told if he could but, unravel the knot he would become ruler of all Asia. He studied the knot, but was unwilling to take the years it might take to successfully unravel the Gordian Knot.

So, he took out his sword, and with one mighty slash cut it open. And, as the story goes, he did become the ruler of all Asia and then some. If sex is our knot, we must cut through it as well, and strike at the truth of the matter. Playing with the knotted issue, only delays our philosophy and moving towards our transformative goals.

A failure to face down this primordial instinct to have sex, to copulate for a progeny, and how it has evolved to occupy and pre- occupy our thoughts has derailed men for generations, over eons. Let's take out our proverbial sword and cut through the myths, and settle on a reality, we can include in our game plans.

RESPECT

Any discussion of sexuality must begin with a core belief. Women deserve respect, and their bodies and sexual choices are sacrosanct. They have an unimpeachable right to say no to sexual advances, and have total control over what sexual acts they will engage, when and with whom, they will consort. All engagements must be of mutual consent, and the woman must be able to respond to requests, free of drugs, alcohol, or other mind altering stimulants.

These restraints include the relationships forged in a workplace, where position and power can influence a coupling. And extends to a group setting, like fraternity housing, where a mob can influence behavior and turn it into dangerous sexual encounters. A society where women have sexual respect and full control of their bodies, is a healthy, democratic environment that fosters equality in all aspects of man to woman contact. The more women are free and at ease in a society the better it is for men to realize relationships that are honest, open, and have clarity and not mixed signals.

Respect also means that men do not seek women merely as conquests, or to satisfy base hormonal impulses. The themes of prior years to "find 'em, feel, 'em, f..k' em, forget ' em," are not only passe', but totally anathema to todays modern code of a relationship.

Each encounter has more at stake than friction, and a biological release of semen.

Any modern game plan would have sexuality in the play book, but would know the limits, purpose, and consequences of actions.

SOCIAL CONTRACT

There is a social contract that brings men and women together for sex. It contains mutual respect, the choice of the woman to say no at any point in the encounter, and for consideration of the feelings and needs of each partner. This bond my seem to be, at first, purely, physical, but it is more than that. Every woman has more than her body parts to bring to a pairing. There is a complex bundle of feelings that are always present that at any moment can explode into something much more meaningful than the moment might suggest. Men have this internal bundle of feelings and hormones as well that drives not only the pairing of the moment, but can evolve into something more profound than a chance encounter.

The initial sexual attraction may emanate from an objectified view of the woman. It is, after all, the essential ingredient in the brew of such desire. And the physical nature of a relationship can sustain a coupling for many outings. But experts who are sexologists to long time escorts account that it is usually for the man much more than just the physical, and objectification that keeps it going. One escort, with over 10,000 encounters accounts that the secret sauce is not her dress, body, or even her special sexual favors. It is instead, someone to support you, free of criticism, who can support your ego, and push away life worries for a few cherished moments. The sex is the lure, but it is not the sustaining force.

POWER ABUSE

Most of us make a living and do our best to create some balance in our lives. Few men would omit sex from their game plan. It may have more influence at some stages of life than others, and when you are in a sexual drought, it can overtake your every thought. But a balanced world view would find it as part of a good life and an additive to any ongoing philosophy. If you are raised to respect women, or adopt that outlook, have average compulsions about sex, and have a complete life otherwise, you will likely not abuse your power over women, in the workplace, or even at home.

But, this is not the case for some men, whose stories of power over women become the fodder of pop culture, movies, and the internet. For some men who know they have control of a career, audition, movie role, or just a job, they are compelled to force women to compromise the obvious 'NO". The nature of these men has given them skills that enabled them to run Hollywood studios, Fortune 500 companies, and hold elected office.

Yet, they do not have to be well known to be abusers. Any man who is lost with his own self esteem issues or unresolved parenting concerns can become a pig and a monster to women who are fearful of rejecting advances.

The cases are diverse and have a scope of psychological malfunctions that are hard to quantify and code. But, most stem from a man who is damaged by his own sense of esteem, or upbringing. Who either hates or reveres women intensely, and forces sex as a validation of his own worth. He my separate this behavior from his overall philosophy and role as provider, philanthropist, or creative force. But, this compartmentalization cannot shield forever what he actually has become, an amoral, twisted man lost in his own distorted world.

They are so lost, they will masturbate before the women, refuse to yield to kisses, touching and fondling. Some actually rape, claiming the sex was consensual. All the while virtually terrorizing the women, some under age, others surprised assistants, advisers and cohorts. Even with new feminism, work rules, and awareness, these actions continue to distort the relationship most men have with woman and the sex they pursue, receive, and honor.

WOMAN AS OBJECT

For a man crafting a philosophy, an obvious stanza would be played that women are not to be viewed as objects. They are complete entities that exist part and apart from their pure physical presence and their ability by cosmic design to satisfy a man's sexual desire and provide the miracle of life. This might appear simplistic, but, it is surrounded by the obvious.

Women are objects, everywhere.

And their beauty, fashion, brains, and rampant sexual appeal, is on all media platforms, and now, ubiquitous on social media. There is no safe haven from women as objects. So when a man ventures towards an attraction based on the obvious,outer shell, he is still chided, ostracized, and screwed.

This cultural shift to an unimpeded self – identification for beauty and surface attributes is part of the post – feminist era. While, they may have this latitude to preen and become the best they can imagine, a man just cannot celebrate that in a vacuum.

A woman can become an object that is outwardly attractive, but, still a man must view her holistically. This is the case regardless of the influence of certain pop culture imperatives that still objectify women, even in the most misogynistic terms, as in rap music, or street poetry. Even, when women self – identify with these images an terms, it is still a mans' role to relate to the entire woman, and foster a relationship from that basis.

Sex flows from an honest approach to looks, sex appeal, and a woman as a person who is a composite of traits that transcend merely the body parts you want to touch and penetrate.

PREVAILING WINDS

There is a shift in the discussion of sexual engagement between men in the workplace, whether that is in Hollywood,

Congress, or your office. The wind blows on all men, making us out to be closet misogynists, serial harassers, or even addicted to sexual couplings. It is a cold wind, as well. Most men are not acting with these aberrant behaviors. It is a small percentage of men who have the above views and act upon them, in violation of any valid ethical code.

The causes of sexual predation, harassment, and/ or addiction are complex and unique to each individual. The roots of these behaviors run deep, and reveal psychosis that is its own Gordian Knot to therapists and sexologists. Healthy sexuality is distorted by a sense of control and power in the case of harassment; predators have compulsions that are fostered by early childhood development anomalies, genetic markers, or late onset mental dysfunction. And sexual addiction presents in a number of anti- social, often compulsive and even violent ways. All are aberrant and outside of the realm of any carefully constructed personal operating philosophy.

As a modern man who has crafted a view of the women in your life, as based upon respect and mutuality in sexual relationships, these prevailing winds will blow past you. But, they are there, and you will need to exercise hyper vigilance to not suggest, imply, or feign that these anomalies represent your views in any manner. And, further, beyond vigilance is the willingness to stop other men from treating woman poorly, and making clear, to even the most powerful and influential men in your life, that such behaviors are forbidden in your presence and with women you know.

THE PRICE OF SEX

Not the sex you pay for from an escort or call girl, but,

the cost of sex to your game plan. Just what are you putting up with, delaying, or avoiding to have a steady sexual life?

Eavesdrop on any conversation between a guy and his gal. Listen in at malls, restaurants or on sidewalks. More often than not, the talk is about what she wants versus what the guy wants. He is often quiet a she rants about her girlfriends, future plans, food, or is into a critique of him, his friends or someone else, or him. And, when you listen, you may wonder why is he putting up with this, and, some of the answer is sex.

Too many men elevate their insecurity about linking up, into allowing compromise on their game plan to stay hooked up to the current woman in their life, even, it means delaying or canning, a life goal to stay with the person in the relationship. If sex was removed from the equation, meaning you could live without it as priority, what types of decisions would you then make about your life goals. If you review what you do to keep her content, and happy enough to have sex with you, is the cost/benefit ratio in babalnce to satisfy your outlook.

Often, what you do, how you act and react, is a direct function of fulfilling her requirements, so she will open the treasure chest, with the "key of approval" she holds over you. This myth that there is a mutuality between men and women about sexual activity, sets men up for the great lie that they have some control over the frequency and desire for sexual interplay. In truth, the modern woman has better cards and more chips in this game.

She asks you to navigate a maze of feelings, conversational stops and starts, and attempt to find the "perfect" mix of timing and emotion to enter the arena of sexual foreplay and the dance to making love. This forces men to spend an inordinate amount of time getting "laid", as part of a recreational and, at times, soulful piece of any relationship. It is a bargain most men make, albeit, grudgingly. And only a few, have the courage to stay on their game plan, and apportion sex to a place that fits time and effort in proportion to its actual worth to their self evolution.

A well considered personal operating philosophy will determine, in any relationship, at anytime, where sex falls in its importance to the relationship and the longer term requirements of the game plan.

To be sure, the scale differs as a man's life goes the natural stages of maturation.

Sex through the Maturation Cycle

Adolescence 13-25

The strongest biological sexual urge occurs in this stage from 13-25. Hormonal imbalance takes over the psyche, and floods the system with testosterone. Peer pressure to "score" also adds to the imbalance. Young men find it difficult to achieve any sense of detachment from the essential drive to orgasm and conquest. And as, it is a formative period for the foundational creation of core values, and long term goals, it is an enormously challenging period to act responsibly in regard to women and sex. The tendency is to objectify women, see them as targets of sexual conquest, and not respond to them as complete beings and/or equals.

This cocktail of hormones and undeveloped moral codes creates the dynamic for abuse and the development of patterns of sexual behavior that can impede more mature relationships throughout a man's lifetime. Fraternity parties, group sex, even drug and alcohol fortified orgies stem from these years. The barriers that are obvious between consent and assault are easily identified, but, as easily violated, as young men allow the women to be seen as vessels and catchers for their semen.

The most powerful method to overcome this instinctive, if onerous behavior, is to encourage a dialogue on the early creation of a Manosphy that respects all women, and relegates sexual escapades to a healthy, but controlled part of a young mans game plan.

Career Fueled 25-45

As a man approaches his mid twenties through the mid-forties, he is likely to be bout establishing his career choices or,at least, pursuing his most likely path to steady income.

Sex, while a driving force of relaxation and health, is not as critical to self –definition as is achieving an income stream, career success, and a sense of momentum towards a purposeful life. In a life where goals are set, and achievements measured, sex becomes a modest driving force, more a 5 than an 8 of the earlier years.

This does not mean that in pursuit of sex, a man will not course correct, alter his goals, or delay them to find a mate, for family creation, or continue to adhere to woman for comfort and solace, as well as, sex. Still it does not define most relationships in this period. The drive to have sex may come as a complement to the achievement of career objectives, as men become exposed to women through work and larger peer groups. Woman are also more engaged in social and sexual by play, as they sample men who may also become long term partners, or even, marriage targets.

This is a period where men can have some emotional and hormonal distance from sex, and begin to place it in perspective in their lives. Here men can ascertain what role sex will play, how much influence will it have, and what are the minimum requirements of placing into their game plan.

Marriage/ Divorce

As men mature so do their relationships in marriage and long term living arrangements. This is not a function of age, as much as lifestyle. Sex becomes a life element that falls precipitously as marriage comes, followed by children, and the full blown array of long term life concerns. That sex survives at all is a tribute to a marriage that requires sex, with enough regularity to offer it as a powerful bond between long term partners.

Besides, finances, sex rules as the source of many breakups.

Through the middle years and beyond, healthy men still require and desire some sex in their lives. Yet, they are less likely to rate as near the top of any fulfilment list. They are more directed towards staying true to themselves and not subjugating their values,self or direction for the moments of friction and pulsations that sex provides. It is an adjunct to love, compassion, and comfort, that are all desired, but have different values to different men, as the age.

For younger men, now one in two in the USA, the long term relationships will end, as men seek new partners for any number of reasons. But, with each new ending and new relationship sex is certainly part of that equation. Often, however, the lack of honesty about the role sex will play can derail these couplings before they get underway. And, their partners may have expectations that need to be surfaced before questions of sex, about how much, when and what are unanswered.

Unfortunately, sex requires more than motion, mechanics, and lubes.

It demands honesty. What does it mean to you. How important is it to you from day to day? What type of sex are you after, and with how many partners? Is sex high or low on your personal list of must haves to fit into your game plan?

The answer to these questions change overtime. Age impacts the answers, as does health, spirituality, and, of course, availability of likeable partners.

Mostly, though the philosophical question rests upon what impact does the pursuit of sex, the constancy of sex have on your life plan. Is it an eternal 8 for you, or a 5. For some its not worth any burden, to put up with the demands and quibbles of a woman just to have a sexual encounter. For others, the pursuit and hope of getting "laid" requires they will suffer any indignity, surmount any emotional obstacle, including spending time with her family to have a few moments of sexual bliss.

Like all of our values, sex demands an assessment. We cannot evolve if we do not know where sex stands now in our game plan.

SEX SCAN

There is no scope to determine the value of sex in your life, no dye that can be injected, or MRI. Instead, you can only scan your beliefs and feelings, rate them, and realize if this fits your transformative process.

On a scale of 1-5, rate each of these:

I find sex is on my mind constantly
Sexual thoughts are rare, but I still have them
I never feel I get enough sex
Sex is often an argument with my partner
When I have sex it is unexciting and boring
I yearn for sex with others
I often fantasize about sex with others
I use pornography as a sex substitute
I consider sex an important part of my life
I need sex more than twice month
I have compromised too much to have sex
Sex is about more than a physical release
I can live without sex and masturbate

Obviously the higher your score, the greater influence sex has on your life, or the lure of it is stronger. But, you can also see how ambivalent your feelings about sex may become as it has les power to pull you off track towards your own life plan. This does not mean that you do not have sexual desire, or enjoy the activity. It does suggest that sex may no longer be a constant in your life. The compulsion you had may have faded,or more likely, has altered as you aged, achieved a career plan, or established longer term relationships.

THE SWORD IS HONESTY

A Manosophy only requires that you have given sex, a place and plan. You still may believe that your goal is to bed as many women as you can. You may believe there is some higher value to being like NBA Hall of Famer, Wilt Chamberlin, who claimed to have screwed 10,000 women. For others, it may a faithfulness to a single woman, as a wife and mother; and to others, a serial array of women, who are respected, and treated morally, with each one offering something to your development.

It is your life plan, your energy and values. Yet, we know that sex has the power to confound and confuse men. It is not a knot easily cut. Our sword is honesty. We do not have Alexander's sword, grace, or mythology. We are merely modern men, in a free society, attempting to treat women properly and ethically, while getting what we want, including sex.

Sometimes the barriers to entry are seemingly too high. We wonder why it is so difficult to have sex, just enjoy the act, and move on. Its complexity can elude men, as it provides release, comfort, and companionship. For, it also requires time, listening, cajoling, gentle persuasion and as many misses as hits. And the partner, may embrace it ever so briefly, in pursuit of control of your actions, desires, and plans.

This myth that women engage in sex for the purity of it, is just that a story of wishful thinking constructed by men. The woman in your life has many influences flowing through her before, during, and after the act of sex. Being in the moment exists in large measure, but dissipates as the next moment fills her mind. We are but along for the ride, and hope, that we get a return ticket. The trick is to not let the desire for more sex, to control us, guide our transformation or worse freeze us in an,otherwise, unsustainable pairing.

What are you prepared to do?

Talk with your partner about role of sex in your life

Review your own history with women in the workplace, are you following rules and boundaries acceptable to you

Is there an instance, where you believe you went too far, and crossed a boundary. What did learn from that encounter.

How would you instruct your son on these issues.?

CHAPTER VIII

What You Would Be Doing If...

"How much time in your life are you giving to planning and preparing for the life you want ?"

Dwayne Dwyer

The reason so few men ever stop to develop a Manosophy or personal operating philosophy is a matter of time. Life seems to move too fast for any consideration of paths, desires, or long term goals. And the last consideration is the evolution of who we are as a person and our innermost desires. No one teaches this self –reflection, it is in no course at college, and is not part of the narrow dialogue men have between each other. It is this very insular approach to our self talk that negates any primary consideration of whether or not we are on the road to happiness, despair, self- actualization or a rutted life .

It is an odd premise to even suggest that the life you are living is so unsatisfying that you should be spending time on what life you actually want to live. But, this is a truism, even for those who engaged in a life that seems to have purpose and offers a degree of fulfilment. When you get quiet, and become reflective, you may find that there is something else you want. It may not be cataclysmic, or grandiose. It could as grounded as more time with your children, coaching after work sports, or driving in an off road race. These are life events and challenges that you want to fit into your life. An accumulation of these new events can add up over time to a fully integrated and new life pattern, if you pursue any of it.

Often men will create ideas, muse about them, and never take the time to figure a way to include in the mix. Then, they become illusory or lost a "to do" list, and the frustration builds as you struggle to get the list done, all the while realizing, nothing is happening. The usual result is the enhancement is forgotten and frustration grows over the years. The addition may require training, new skills, or a chunk of time, and you are unprepared to put aside the current life for the other life.

When the changing force is truly life altering, men will set goals, reverse engineer their time lines, and create incremental steps to accomplish the task. If you want to be a lawyer, you take the course, study, find a school, and develop a plan to pay for it and find the time to do it all. A mechanic who wants to be a firefighter does the same, or a science teacher who sets his sights on becoming a doctor.

The pathway is the same. Each with its own specific timeframe and trajectory. But all share the same elements.

Sighting and Targets

If you took inventory of your current activities, you would find a full agenda. Yet, there is most likely any number of activities or new directions you would take, if you knew you could not fail at any attempt. This fear of failure in new ventures is the primary impediment to change, but it need be overwhelming. The way to test these activities mundane or global is to first determine your target as you see it and then take incremental steps to achieve the result you are seeking.

It begins with setting a sight on that activity, event, idea or dream that currently compels you to take some action. The best definition of the sighting may be driven by an event or cluster of activities that will get you moving in the direction you wish to proceed.

For example; you may wish to become an endurance athlete. You sign up for a marathon, six months away.

You always had an interest in being a chef. You sign up for culinary classes.

You want to be a nurse. You enter a two year associate degree program.

These sightings get you in motion. They force you out of the current work, play, rest pattern, and require you offer some time to the new activity.

These activities then become part of a targeted effort, if you decide to pursue a full life change. Once targeted, you establish a schedule, a timeline, and begin to act as though you have already achieved the transformation. The power of action when joined an imagination fueled by seeing yourself in the end circumstances, will assist in rocketing you towards the new persona you are seeking.

Yet, just as that creating a list, day dreaming about it,

will yield you only regrets, if you take no action. A sighting offers a sense of momentum, but, is static in actuality. You see what you wish to do, target it, do it, and then decide if you should continue.

It may be your last marathon or one of many. You may take a few courses on becoming a nurse, and then drop it. And you may really want to become a world class chef and have no real aptitude for any of it. But each effort expands you, and allows to strike freely at your stake on happiness, bliss, and fulfilment .

Failing to sight new things, finding no targets for expansion, leaves you where you are now. And, that place may be enough, for the game plan of your life. The only judgment to be offered is your own of your philosophy.

If You Could Not Fail .. and Reality

It is, of course, a parlor game, this "if you could not fail" concept. It is a challenge designed to force free thought about an undetermined future. Cognitively, it requires little but imagination and a light spirit. The purpose is to open your mind to possibilities without regard for neither failure nor ability and aptitude.

The Exercise

Sit by yourself and ask the question, "what would I be doing now, If I could not fail"

Without regard for reality based upon any criteria, write down the answer, and do not censor your thoughts. Just write them down.

For example, "Climbing Everest", means I want to seek adventure and be a mountaineer.

Row the Pacific- take a voyage, that most would think impossible, but can be done

Lounging in Tahiti- a desire to take exotic, get away trips

Driving at Daytona-wanting to be involved in racing cars, or following them

Running a Food bank- be a community asset

Write as many scenarios as you can imagine, some will have heart, others will be the stuff of a male fantasy life, write them all down. Hopefully, the exercise has released you from that narrow minded, stuck, mind set we all develop. Here is an opportunity at no cost or consequence to say what you would be doing, no matter how frivolous or tough to achieve.

Now go back over the responses and weigh the value of the responses, in regard to these factors:

What am I yearning for: a new beginning or new activities?

Are these activities of escape and just new experiences or do they reflect a deeper need

What do they tell me as a cluster of new experiences.

Is what I want to be doing a subset of what I am doing or is it a departure?

If I actually pursued these things, what would I become?

Is this exercise meaningful or am I content with my current circumstances and life goals?

Often this game seems useless and without merit. We are so often tied to the status quo that any consideration of a different future path seems just frivolous. Yet, how can we sight a different future, target new things, without some probing. Most, never ask any question about their path, never establish a game plan, have no operating philosophy.

For these men, who are the majority, life proceeds along a path set in motion by some purpose or the purpose of someone else. Life meanders from work, to family responsibility, some play, and avoids wrestling with this seminal issue of "is this the life you want".

This is not an all or nothing analysis. There are parts of life that will fit into a developing philosophy, some that are there and must be managed and maintained, and others that are holding you back from achieving the life you are actually after. Whether you can activate your plan is a function of your view of past achievements and the attributes you bring to the tasks.

Achievement and Attributes

There is an inventory worthy of consideration that will assist in this review of the life you are living, and reveal what aspects my need to be jettisoned. No matter what your age, or circumstances you have already amassed a significant cluster of achievements. Further, these accomplishments are only what you have achieved with your skills and personal power. These same attributes can open the way to new paths and the exploration of this life now defined by your personal operating system.

The achievement pattern is diverse, but, includes completing education milestones, beginning career choices, and blending activities that provide excitement, underline interest, and a sense of accomplishment. Everyone has their own checklist, and, it can reveal how you are developing towards your own self- definition. But, these same achievements may also be the mark of success that is not about what you want. This gap between what you are getting done and what you want to get done is the source of growing grief in a mans life. While you are buoyed by the success, it can still be hollow.

The key here is to review each effort and assess it against this criteria:

Did my achievement here satisfy my goals or the goals of someone else?

And if the goal was satisfying to you, what debate it bring on with others. Simply, is what you are doing causing friction with others in your life. If so, what is the source of the disconnect? Sometimes, it is the amount of effort and time, you must give to accomplish a task or earn a living, that alone causes the disconnect. Achievement takes, time, effort, and energy that can leave little for anything else. Are you being blamed for not being more balanced?

This lack of balance is a theme of the lives of most men. Work occupies time and is a requirement of income generation, professional or tradesmen growth, and a sense of worth in the world. Often, the critique of men comes from women, out of this reality. And the avocations require as much time, if not more.

Yet, if you deny yourself the trip to the ball game, or delay the fishing trip, or don't take the time to paint, change out an engine, hike a trail, you are cheating yourself. There are bucket lists for all manner of activities that may fill up your tank of accomplishments. Denial of any of that diminishes you, and stops a flow of energy that may reveal new directions for you.

The narrow life, lived in a rutted trail, yields just that, no more.

Achievement is about expansion. You can have a philosophy that allows for rugged individualism, which is not selfish or exclusionary. This means that you have goals that are about work, recreation, and, also, solitude. That this my include others from family and children, or it may not. Doing what you must, and doing what you desire are not insular, anti- social acts. Yet, there is a outlook that men who live life with an expansive game plan are not in touch with reality. The reality, you seek, is the one that reinforces your outlook, code, and operating philosophy, not the critiques views.

So, what have you achieved? What is ahead ?

Health and Fitness

Do feel fit and at peak health, are you robust, at a reasonable weight, and active enough to meet your life goals

Education

Have you accomplished the terminal degree or training needed to succeed, or is more required or desired, if you change your path and direction

Job

Is this current job providing the income, and stability you need? Is it a step towards a future or is it time to move on, or at least change, locations. Are you engaged and still fulfilled day to day?

Career

Does the job seem to offer career prospects? If you spent the time on getting into this career choice, does it still compel you? Is there more you can achieve, and in what time frame that you accept

Avocations- high interest pursuits

Have you established some outlets for your interest, that define other aspects of your persona? Should you explore other activities that may further expand you, or delete some to find time for others?

Family

What role and priority does the family play in your game plan? Is it the driving force of your work and income generation? Are you offering enough time and presence to have an impact?

Children

How much are you in their lives? When you are with them are you truly present?

What guidance are you providing in school, activities and associations?

Faith and Spirit

. Are you practicing a faith? How are you participating in the pursuit of tenets of that belief system? Do you find you are more or less attached spiritually to your world, and others. You believe in something, are you acting affirmatively to protect your beliefs?

Possessions

Are there some things you use as a marker of success? The car, living space, guns, collectibles? Do you have a checklist of other things that you value, that you still want to have,but yet to own.

Wealth

Do you believe you are accumulating wealth ? Is the

rate of growth in keeping with your short term (savings) and long term (retirement) goals? What actions can you take to enhance your wealth?

Personal development

As a person are you evolving ? Can you control your emotions, not be distracted by drama, set goals? Do you find yourself more pleased with your accomplishments, than stressed? Is there a point each day, when you feel content or at peace with yourself?

Are you frayed most days and spent or do you feel fatigue from time well spent?

These questions suggest the direction you will take to enhance what you have already achieved and drive you to consider a list of what is next. Each aspect suggests a way forward that must be based upon your timing, and an approach to development and change that does not further stress and crush your willingness to alter your life plan.

Attributes

Each of us has a distinct set of attributes that are derived from our upbringing, innate of genetic makeup, and our learning experiences. No one is frozen to a set of skills. You are not, so called, destined to be what you now are until death. You can select a different path, amend the one you are on, or strike out, cogently towards another destination. These attributes can suggest a way forward, but cannot predict the end result. Through an awareness of the traits that comprise your make- up,you can begin an assessment of what you might alter, keep, or improve upon.

Natural

The impact of genetics on our natural attributes is often obvious. These imbedded traits are woven into our DNA and present themselves as we develop. While, you may desire to be a world class surfer, you may be stymied by a lack of balance. A tennis player with limited eye hand co-ordination, or a NBA player if you have height, coordination, and muscle power. These physical capabilities can translate to activities that help define your life choices. More complex genetic markers that involve patience, warmth, communication skills, introverted and extroverted, all seem to have some genetic disposition.

Overcoming physical attributes can be achieved by hard word, adaption, and setting realistic goals. Yet, even in this regard, a man can overcome most physical deficits, or find a substitute activity. Sometimes the most seemingly insurmountable physical or talent barrier can be overcome by the attribute of persistence, stubbornness, and commitment. You can run a 100 mile race, play baseball for a AAA team, or swim around Manhattan Island, if you use your acquired attributes to overcome genetic flaws.

Genetics is not wholly destiny. Even, the expression of certain genetic markers of disease, and weakness have remedy. And, you may find you have other, non physical, but attitudinal traits, like pessimism that can be a challenge, as you fight to redefine your overall outlook.

If talent is a gift, then the development of character is a choice.

The list of natural attributes will reveal some of who you are, and why you are the person you have become to some extent. But, it is not immutable, in fact you will find that you can use some character traits to overcome or diminish attributes that are seemingly permanent but can be managed towards your goals.

The only real obstacle to growth and your success at creating a Manosophy, is doing nothing. If you take what you are given, adopt a viewpoint of acceptance, you may cut off possibilities that are within your grasp. Of course, the view that "this is who I am, "screw it", is also a viewpoint, that may suit you, especially if you are blessed with a composite of traits that prove to provide purpose, cash flow, and some degree of happiness.

There are so few of us,who fit into the subset of extremely talented men, who pursue a life that is based upon their physical and mental natural talents. For the rest of us, who are not Heisman candidates, it is a struggle. Bodybuilding great, and Incredible Hulk star, Lou Ferrigno, suffered hearing loss, and self doubt, even as he found solace and spiritual power in lifting weights. Men who have nothing from the gene pool, in some things, have countervailing attributes in others. And, often, character traits are an attribute than can trump genetic influences.

Other Attributes

Most of us use this reservoir of behavioral traits as our source of influences that drive our actions. These traits may be partially inborn, or developed as a response to stimuli as we matured. You may have no natural patience, but you developed it, out of necessity to grow in your job. Your outlook may be trusting, which you amended to "trust, but verify" after being hurt on business deals. Each trait inherent or acquired becomes part of a collection of attributes, you bring to situations and life choices.

Attributes need be forced into a single outlook or philosophy. Often these traits are all required as tools to accomplish goals, not as rote parts of a frozen personality. Being tough, is helpful in business dealings, and in discipline of others, it neither good nor bad. It is the application and use of the trait that presents its meaning. Being tough and still being warm and empathetic is a composite of traits that may fit your personal operating philosophy.

How might these traits combine to provide the tools you need to create a resilient and productive personality fueled by a transformed outlook.

Introvert/ Extrovert

Are you more open or closed. Do you find you are more comfortable with others or most happy and productive in solitary pursuits.

Open

Are you by nature open to ideas and the thoughts of others

Conscientiousness

Do you get things done, by staying with projects. You are tenacious, accountable, reliable

Agreeable

Easy to get along with, open minded, more positive than negative. People seem to enjoy being with you

Neurotic

Do you obsess on projects, get overly dramatic, to the point of wearing down family and associates.

From these basic, and traditional psychological definitions, what other traits do you have in some measure, that can help define your best path towards the life you want to plan.

Do you exhibit the following traits or attributes, on some regular basis:

Do you keep PROMISES

How LOYAL are you to friends and family

Are you seen as HONEST about everything, with consistency

How HARD DRIVING are you in pursuit of dreams, goals, others needs

Is being KIND and WARM to others on your list of traits

Can you be TOUGH when required to impose discipline or situation or people

Do you see and treat everyone as EQUALS

Is there enough energy or STAMINA within you, so you have the energy meet commitments

How HARDY are you? Can you get knocked down, even when faced with injustice and get up, again and again

Is there a perspective on life, that you hold within you that includes taking events in stride and with some sense of appropriate HUMOR.

When you put these traits together with your inherent attributes, you begin to see a cluster of traits that currently defines who you are and how you appear to the world. You may find it unacceptable in some areas, and perfect in others. What really matters is how these clusters assist you in creating a personal operating philosophy that meets your requirements, and brings enjoyment, happiness, and purpose to your game plan.

Figuring out what you would be doing, if you could fail, can be a solitary pursuit. You inventory what we have discussed, list your attributes and your wishes, and then backtrack the process to determine what you must do, in increments, to achieve the goals.

We know that such seminal change begins with an imaging in our mind of what we wish to become. Then, we begin to act as though we are already at our imagined destination. Simply, if you want to be a lawyer, start dressing, speaking, and acting as if you are already there. And then once accomplished begin again, imagining, acting, and doing what you see in your philosophical mirror.

All this can be accomplished without others or their guidance.

Yet, for some the process accelerates, when combined with these factors:

Best Minds

There are other men with thoughts like yours. They may be in groups, or in settings for learning, like institutes, universities, or places where what you want to learn or become is what they are doing. Showing up, absorbing ideas, will help generate, the positive feedback you need to go forward and not give up in your pursuit of change.

Other self help gurus call this Master Minds, Super Thinkers, it is the same idea, and costs you nothing. Feed your interest with the best minds in the area of interest.

Mentor Man

There are men who want to help and teach. Some do it for cash, most for the joy of helping another guy find himself professionally or personally. Sometimes just a friend is so wise, as to offer insights you are seeking. Other times, you will need to find men who are already expert in their field, and they will offer some guidance. Unpaid, mentors should be accessed on occasion or at a crossroads, the paid you can have a more regular schedule. Smart men want to mentor others, it helps them grow, and is an offering of sustaining value.

Drop the Losers

Just as you must imagine yourself as you want to be, and you throw out old clothes, and toss away old habits, you must also lose people who are remnants of the past. This does not mean that good friends or family should be discarded. But it does mean that there are people from your other life that offer little to your new outlook. There is no reason to be unkind, but relationship can mature to a point where it is better that they fade, and not occupy time and effort needed for the next phase. This will happen naturally, but, you must face this reality, moving forward will not allow for you to pull along a cart of old friends and acquaintances, at least not with any regularity

Creating a game plan is not about dreaming. It is not only about imaging a future life. You can inventory your wishes, assess your attributes, generate a bucket list, and still decades later lived a narrow and rutted life. The difference, of course, is developing a philosophy that empowers you to change and transform yourself. And this requires action and planning. This is the essential ingredient of a game plan, a playbook that offers goals, preparation and execution to win at your life.

What are you prepared to do?

What would you be doing right now, if you could not fail?

Inventory these attributes:

Natural

Traits

Create timelines and Incremental Action plan, for imaginary new pursuits

CHAPTER IX

The Playbook

You do not need a playbook that is telephone book size. What you want are some keys that you can execute, no matter what, anywhere, and against anyone.

Coach Charlie Martin
Northeast High 1962

It is in vogue today for even high school quarterbacks to lug round playbooks of considerable size and weight. There are so many plays, with so many scenarios that QB's now have wrist bands with the plays on them. The day of "Stosh up the middle", etched out in the turf at a two hand touch game, is long gone. Still, the Coach Martin's were not wrong that a few plays well executed could win most games. Life does throw scenarios at us that are unknown, or so unique we cannot anticipate their arrival. And, we have the assets to reach our goals with some preparation, planning, and luck.

OUTCOME ANALYSIS

Most problems are more easily conquered, if you adopt an approach to them based upon OUTCOMES. This means that when you face any issue or challenge, you take a pause and consider what result you are after BEFORE you act. This forces you to review your options to accomplish the goal and directs your energy and skills towards the end game you desire. Often, we are so involved and attached to the problem that we act on impulse, passion, or narrow self – interest. We may achieve the outcome we are after, but it often happens only after we have created even more obstacles to our success.

This type of analysis can assist in winning advantage in global concerns and the mundane. You want to buy a high rise building, that is the outcome and at a certain price. Obviously, you must decide for how much and with what financing. If you know the end game, you can take steps to maneuver your opponent and strike the deal you require. On a smaller scale, you want to acquire a classic truck, at a price you have researched, you cannot get it, if you impulsively argue with the owner, and haggle, to a price point he will not accept. Or, you must fire an employee, but you want him to walk away with his self- esteem intact, how do you get to that outcome?

REVERSE ENGINEER IT

All outcomes that you design and desire can be achieved, if you also reverse engineer what you must do to get there. There are steps towards any outcome. You decide the outcome and then review all the steps you must take to get there in the most linear process available. To be sure, even the most well planned approach may require an adaption based upon timing, or a need to alter direction based upon the response of other players. You can misread your opponent, underestimate an adversary, or misjudge who is in your corner. All of these factors can derail your field of play. But, you have a much better chance of getting it done, your way, once you reverse the steps from outcome to starting point.

The pattern is the same for any scenario:

State the Outcome: Run a Marathon in November

Reverse Engineer the Steps: 120 days to train, build mileage gradually; do three 20 mile runs, change diet to more carbs, raise money for charity, change daily routine

Obstacles: family time may be cut, negative feedback from spouse, chronic Achilles pain, travel for work, staying motivated

Strategy to overcome obstacles

Incentives to achieve goal: pride, sense of accomplishment, superior fitness, bucket list.

Not all plays are as volitional as running a marathon. Plays that come from a deep sense of meaning or accomplishment are often the easiest to achieve, regardless of their level of difficulty. It is the other life plays like getting married, having a family, that seem more daunting, and they are by any measure. The complexity comes from a lack of linearity, and the impact of the forces that surround the play. Often the list of obstacles can seem as daunting as going from Everest base camp to the summit. They require not only outcome analysis, but a will to succeed, and a determination to complete and run this life play, regardless of difficulty, obstacles, or what it takes out of you energetically.

But, these life plays also require more than will and energy. They all require a commitment of the spirit within you as well. It may be driven by a faith, or just a belief you have that this play must be executed, and your spirit helps drive you forward. There is no play, on any field of play, that is not assisted by this inner yearning. Spirited players are more likely to succeed. Even less skilled athletes can rise above their attributes and beat larger, sifter rivals, if their spirits are joined towards the same outcome.

If your life play is driven by your willfulness, purpose, and possessed of an undaunted spirit, you will execute that play, and be less drained for the efforts.

DO THIS BEFORE YOU TAKE ON ANY PLAY

Take each play in your life, and apply the above principles. What is my outcome? What steps must I take to achieve it? Reverse engineer that process. What are the obstacles? How can I deal with the obstacles? What incentives do I have to stay on course and execute this play?

You already have the most essential tools as you have developed your MANOSOPHY. You have decided upon a personal operating philosophy, adopted an outlook that fits your persona, and reviewed your attributes and skills, and are steely to fight the horseman of shame, guilt, fear, and approval.

Perhaps, after all of this your manosophy is still, "Shit Happens", or perhaps, you have decided that whatever happens you can deal with it, because you have skills and are resilient, or, your destiny and life is your own hands and with good deeds and faith, you will chart a better life. In any case your personal operating philosophy is now yours and designed to transform you, guide you, and enhance your life potential.

Hopefully, you have adopted an outlook that is more optimistic, that enables you to be hardy as you fight obstacles, and gives you enormous power to fight back against injustice, curves in your road, and jerks. You know that by having such an outlook, you have distinguished yourself from others who just accept what is happening to them, or are committed to pessimism as a crutch in their lives.

You know that what you think impacts all of your actions. Further you are prepared to filter what you say, so when you speak you have power, influence and good spirit when you can. And you save speech that is critical, and instructive for those moments when it is most needed and will have impact. You also have considered what you now put in your mouth, and, whether it has value of nutrition, just taste, or to fill an emotional hole.

In some measure, you have come to question your sense of faith and the role it plays in your philosophy. And your awareness of the horsemen of despair that can hold you back and derail your dreams; shame, fear, guilt, and the quest for approval is acute. With all your skills, your enhanced awareness of an examined life's power, you are well prepared to consider these life plays.

PLAYS

ON THE JOB – The Next Move

A play that comes in most career paths is the need to advance in a profession or job choice. While the jobs we have are diverse, the same standards can be applied towards getting to the goal of job advancement.

All plays begin by with the definition of the play. In this case:

The Play:

Advance job prospects through promotion, more responsibility and with enhanced compensation.

Outcome: better job position and more income or stock

Reverse Engineer: successful goal achievement on some incremental level; spend some time with decision- maker to allow for interpersonal rapport; present new ideas or enhance existing themes; put in time on clock and off to learn new skills or hone existing ones.

Obstacles: other colleagues with more verbal or socialization tools; poor corporate relationships; clash of ideology or personality clashes; unscrupulous rivals

Strategy : make work product better known; spend time on management skills; seek mentors; play by ethical rule book.

Set a realistic time frame for advancement and establish guidelines for exit strategy.

Incentives: personal advancement, enhance self esteem, generate cash flow for future security, start family, or plan retirement.

RELATIONSHIPS

The Play : Find a steady, exclusive, person that may be foundation for marriage and family

Outcome: long term relationship and family

Reverse Engineer: Become committed to fulfilling work, and positive work environment. Spend time in avocational pursuits, that allows circulation to women outside of work. Continue to stay connected to family units and extended family to serve as source for meeting others. Be more well rounded in interests, and activities.

Obstacles: afraid of commitments, ambiguity over family life, overly work focused; unresolved family issues on marriage and children, parental dismay. Peer pressure to stay single.

Strategy: See more women, visit target rich environments, be open to short term but exclusive relationship. Be more verbal, open, and listen as much as you speak to the women in your life. Use family and friends to offer and provide introductions.

Incentive: a rich personal life includes a significant other, who embraces your goals and dreams. Such a person offers more than solace and warmth, but also support, encouragement and, even the prospect, of children and a legacy.

This is a play that most men face, and it is as complex as any you might ever encounter. Certainly, few men are as calculating about this play, as others, but some thought, a diagram of what you are thinking can help. This Thought Mapping™ can guide you towards the destination, but, we are not unrealistic and deluded. The "forces" will intercede and it will require all our hardiness, and optimism to complete this play.

LOSS

The play: loss comes into the lives of all men. How to cope, recover, and move on.

The approach to all loss can be Thought Mapped, but it is tempered by what is lost, the severity of the loss if it is family member, the time in life the person passes, and where you are in your own transformation. The landscape of loss is a mural, filled with dark hues and some light. It is the goal of this play to embrace the darkness, and eventually let the light warm you over time.

Outcome: To emerge with understanding, emotionally under control, and able to go forward, not stymied by the loss, or allow it to occupy my every thought.

Reverse Engineer: review the person's role in your life, establish the best memories in your mind through discussion or collection of memories in photos, text, or objects, seek others to work through the stages of grief. Seek the wisdom of your faith or belief system. Practice forgiveness and consciously decide to heal, with no definite timeframe.

Obstacles: Unresolved issues with deceased. Others dictating your feelings. No time to mourn due to crush of work, or other concerns. Emotionally unable to face the loss, at this point in your life. Too many other negative events or challenges at the time of the loss. Inability to settle yourself.

Strategy: allow time to pass, do not feel need to immediately resolve all feelings. Spend time with your thoughts, and approach yourself gently, and with compassion. You are responsible for your thoughts, feelings and actions. Take each moment, as a victory, and overtime resolve what this loss means, or not, to your transformation.

Incentives: to seize the reality of the loss, but, not exorcise the spirit of the person you lost. They are either with you, or not when needed. Some you may expunge ., not everyone has the same grip or influence on our lives. But, the execution of this play is ultimately to be a peace with the loss, and use its force to move you forward.

BE EPIC- The Big Play

The Play- pursue an activity that is unexpected, larger than life, risky and bold

The Outcome: go for a project, set goal, that is by design Epic in scope and accomplishment. Physical or intellectual.

This is the type of extraordinary that most men avoid, as life envelopes them. But, everyman can have an epic effort or many in their gameplan. A big play can rejuvenate a job, reinforce a life pursuit, or just energize and refocus your current way of thinking.

Some examples of big plays would include massive, collaborative efforts like, President John Kennedy committing to landing a man on the moon, to individual triumphs, like Sir Edmund Hilary and Tensing Norgay climbing Everest in 1953. All required the same outcome analysis, we are applying here. But, all started with a drive to be epic, to think big, and find a way.

Everyone who thinks epic, has the same insight. It is, you can always find a way. This does not mean you will succeed at first, or even 20,000 light bulbs later, just ask Thomas Edison. For Diana Nyad, it took multiple swims, to finally swim from Cuba to Florida.

And collective efforts require more than desire, and careful planning, Super Bowl wins are still rare, and often not obvious, ask any Las Vegas bookie.

If you are a billionaire, you have the luxury of being epic. Yet, few do. Elon Musk builds electric cars, creates battery farms, send rockets to the space station, and thinks we all should ride in tubes to work. Crazy? Epic? A guy named,Carl Fisher, saw sand in South Florida and turned the sand and swamp into Miami beach, and reaped a fortune.

But you do not need capital to realize epic goals. You need a will to leap from the day to day and do something that will for all time define you. Row across the Pacific, run 135 miles through the Mojave Desert; start a homeless shelter; turn coffee drinking into a billion dollar business; be a Big Brother; or start an afterschool program for boxing and computer learning.

It is about not thinking with limits, and allowing your

philosophy to encompass the outlier thought and the time to find the big goal, undaunted by the day to day.

Outcome: accomplish an outlandish task, or goal. Stretch myself towards the most epic goal I can imagine

Reverse Engineer: What does this require in terms of physical capacity or intellectual preparation? Have I already experienced some of this in smaller form or for less duration? What is the calendar, needed to properly prepare and plan for the goal? What is the cost/benefit ratio to achieve this goal? Are the earning increments gradual enough to train, prepare, practice and execute ?

Obstacles: time to prepare and plan; funds required to pursue ; critique of family and friends of efforts; boss feeling this is taking too much energy and is a distraction from my work. Do my capabilities enable me to achieve this epic task?

Strategy: select epic adventure that complements skill sets; create long term calendar, that allows for fits and starts; be prepared for many frustrations in preparation and execution; establish goal with others in like pursuits for support, advice, and mentoring

Incentive: the rush of doing something epic. The financial reward if the entrepreneurial spirit succeeds. An addition to my life, that is memorable, and once accomplished cannot be taken away. It becomes part of my self –definition.

THE DEMONS COME

The play: overcoming the reality of the forces; job loss, injury, dreams blown.

No matter how well you plan nor how righteous your

intentions, plans fail, people let you down, collaborators fade, and the forces descend upon your outcomes.

Fighting back and rebounding requires the same outcome analysis. In fact, when under the stress of these forces, it is all the more essential to establish some emotional distance from the derailment, so you can establish an approach to cope and move on.

Job loss is a constant for most men. Whether it is imposed or by choice. There are periods in this new digital age, when you will be between steady, employment and income. The life long job, is rare, and is the reason many men are seeking jobs that offer more self- sufficiency, flexible hours, and the opportunity to develop other skills and earning paths outside of traditional work environments.

Even onto the most stable paths, injury and accidents occur. These pauses in productivity and wellness can have a devastating impact on a man's sense of purpose and self. The goal here is to limit the impact of the unexpected event, so its potential for damage is lessened.

Then there may be a reckoning ; you may work for a specific goal, or even a dream, and a life altering event can change the direction of your life. You may have an injury that stops your athletic career, a family loss that requires you to be close to home, or you realize the skills you have will not enable you to succeed at your chosen endeavor. This composite of realizations can leave you lost, or thrust towards an even more energetic future, albeit, with a new set of goals and directions.

All of the above are a type of loss, of course. But unlike the loss of a life, they all suggest a rebirth and a recrudescence, if you allow it to happen.

Thus:

Outcome : to regroup after job loss, injury, or end of dreams

Reverse Engineer: what was the causation of the event? Did I play any role in the approach of these forces? Was there some karmic thrust to these events? If I replay the events leading to this; was I fatigued, angry, lost, upset, or off my game enough to have contributed subconsciously to this result? Was there a crossroads event that, if I had chosen differently this result was avoided? What role did volition play here?

Obstacles: letting go of the perception that I was responsible for the loss? If I had a role, was I acting ethically and with clarity? Co- workers and loved ones may negate my recovery, and urge a return to prior lifestyle. Loss of psychic energy to regroup in short timeframe. Need to find income quickly.

Strategy: make assessment of reason for loss; move towards new plan for income, in short and long term. Rehab on reasonable schedule, and be determined to not force recovery; do a full skill review to determine if you should return to fulfilment of larger goals or strike out in another direction that is congruent with your personal operating philosophy. If you need a new gameplan, create it as you heal.

Incentives: a reboot of your work, as you regain your wellness. Your hardy outlook and overall philosophy will drive you towards the continuation of self – improvement and the transformation of a better life you seek. This recovery fuels that quest.

Thought Mapping

Throughout the process of being outcome oriented, and selecting an approach to problem solving, the tool of thought mapping has value. It releases your mind to actually visualize options and approaches. All great playbooks are mapped by a coach or planner. In football you see X's and O's. They complexity and permutations of a NFL playbook are legion, but all start with a thought map, or mind map.

It is about having a thought and placing it in the center of a blank sheet of paper. Then lay down your reverse engineering criteria in other clusters. Take the time to chart out your steps to accomplish the outcome. Put them around the outcome on the page. Give major steps larger size, and smaller increments smaller ones.

Then map out clusters of obstacles, and write other obstacles as they come to your thought process. If they are major, make them bigger, smaller challenges less so.

Your thought map now has a main outcome, a series of clusters of incremental steps to take to accomplish the task, and a cluster array of obstacles. Now on the perimeter of this mapping, write in clusters of strategies you will employ to attack the obstacles and clear the way for success.

This paper now has on it, your play, outlined as your mind works. One thought leading to another, but channeled by the discipline of the process. You can then translate this process into direct bullet points on your phone on wherever you keep your notes.

A journal of these plays makes sense, since it is actually your philosophical playbook. Over time this playbook will grow and offer you insights into every major play you had to execute in keeping with you Manosophy.

OWN YOUR LIFE

George Leonard, one of the founders of the spiritual retreat, Esalen, was also a master of Aikido. It is a marshal art that uses an opponents force and intention as a weapon to redirect energy and motion. In Aikido, you blend with the attackers force and then assess and strike. It is a flowing, almost imperceptible method of defense, and its precepts to Leonard are a mark of how to live a fulfilling life and meet obstacles. In his revolutionary, The Way of Aikido, he posits that the most critical task of a person, especially a novice is to "own your Mat".

How much life are you wasting, being tentative. There is no action, none that is enhanced by being so,so. A tennis player wins when they are in control of their game, attacking and retreating as needed. Being all out and committed does not men being constantly aggressive, being mean- spirited, or attacking with abandon, at all. It means knowing what actions you must take, and taking them with your full and complete life force.

This can be expressed with finesse, charm, softness, and gaiety. At other times, it is about the show and use of enormous power in a bat swing, a forehand smash, or a right hook. But, owning your life, is owning your mat. You walk into it, prepared to do what you must to hold it. You are centered, confidant, aware of your skills, and unattached to any single encounter or outcome.

Life lived this way, all out and totally committed is richer, textured, and fulfilling. Have you ever seen a skier who is tentative? They are so concerned about the totality of hitting a tree, they hit the tree. Their focus is not on enjoyment, learning, and transcendence. They have forgotten that in life, philosophy and skiing, it is always about,"one turn at a time."

The best performers, the most enlightened, know that you can only control and deal with this moment. As you link one focused moment to another, a miracle happens. You begin to enjoy life, reach goals, and are resilient to change, and failures.

This playbook is precisely about that reality. You must have a playbook, formed from your attack on the events of your life. You can adapt to change, alter approaches and outcomes by the use of all your traits, your consciousness and unconscious mind. If you are prepared to be aware of your goals, channel your thoughts, and stay true to your philosophy,you will OWN YOUR LIFE.

What are you prepared to do?
Lay out Thought maps for your current plays
Log your plays in your own playbook
Test the theory on a few plays
Assess your outcomes

Select an area of your life where you are being tentative and change your behavior.

CHAPTER X

Man Circles

In the Circle of Life /it is the wheel of fortune/it is the leap of faith/' til we find our place/on the path unwinding/in the circle/ The Circle of Life

Elton John

The challenge of the examined life, is not just to know what you want, and plotting a strategy to get there. It is,also, about how to create a day that includes the activities encompassed by your gameplan. You are not a writer, if you only imagine your text; not a sailor who dreams of the ocean; not a teacher, if you only speak to yourself. This is such an obvious observation, yet, how many men, actually spend time, of any substantial measure doing what will give them the life they desire. You cannot transform yourself, only through your imagination, action is required. This apportionment of time need not be immediate or overtake, the life you are living, but, increments are needed to eventually re-cast the time you spend doing activities that define your life.

If you draw a circle of your life, charting how much time you spend in certain pursuits, what will it reveal? Often men are chided for living unbalanced lives. The people who claim this are often those who want more attention, and time from you. All the while, you may agree with this critique, but you have little power to alter the arrangement since the "have to" outweigh the "want to".

In fact, at certain stages of a mans' development, as in a career spurt or the start up of a new enterprise, the unbalanced, work oriented, life is prudent. Some men find that the balanced life of work, family, rest, recreation is boring, and rutted. There is no perfect circle of life, that can be imposed by anyone but you, as it fits your personal operating philosophy. What matters is that it is congruent with your desire to evolve, and grow into a happier, purposed existence. The life circle you chose will also change, as activities, challenges, and circumstances dictate. But, the key to Manosophy is to create that balance that fits the path you chose, in Elton John's words, on "that path unwinding".

The Man Circle

This is a straight forward, no bull way to monitor what you are doing and where you are going. It is based upon the ability we all have to draw a circle. You can do this on a napkin, in the ground at the worksite, or on your laptop. How you draw it does not matter. That you do it, does.

You draw the circle and then fill in the elements or

activities that define your life. There are three circles for you to draw, as time passes.

Circle 1- what you are doing and how you apportion your activities NOW

Circle 2- A future circle,whenever you seek to check on progress, how different is this from the last circle

Circle 3-The Ideal- what you hope to have as your life, as you progress towards the fulfilment of your personal operating philosophy .

Circles will be different in proportion based upon the workweek. You will have a circle for the workweek and one for off time. But, even the off work circle, should change as you evolve.

We will explore three (3) circles. The workweek and life balance; the relationship between your mind, body, and soul; and, the perfect hour at work.

BASICS

Man Circles include activities that are Have To and Want To Do. If you are honest, you will likely find that, as you draw your circles, and include elements, you will see most days more HAVE's, and on weekends or on vacation the Want To Do's. The most rare elements allow for reflection, contemplation, and planning for the future. It is a cluster of elements that are REQUIRED for the nurturing of the man you will become, without it, you are spinning in place, and your intentions are going to take much longer to be revealed.

So what are your basic activities and elements, first in an average day.

Now- Draw a Circle

Insert these elements based upon the time you spend each day, if they don't exist in your day, exclude them

Work

Family/ girlfriend/ children

Rest/sleep

Recreation/workout/sports activity

RCP (reflection, contemplation, planning for future)

Prayer/faith/ meditation/silence

Review the Circle you just created:

That is enough for this basic exercise. What does your circle contain? Does it seem to fulfill your needs, and does it allow for what you want to be doing? If the recreation is one hour and you want it to be more on some days, you must begin to plot a strategy to make it so. If you take no steps, and accept the man circle, it will not change. There is no magic here.

If want the segments to change, you have to decide what will change, and on what timetable.

ENRICHED MAN CIRCLE

The elements of a circle are enhanced by volition. You want more, or less of what you have experienced most of your days. You find that as you act as if you are the man you want to become, activities change. This is an individual choice, of course, the artist must spend time at the canvas, the surfer on his board, the doctor with his patients. The key is to redraw these circles as your life changes. The basic circle of today, pulsates with new influences and response to change.

The key is to draw the circle each month, check your instincts of how much time you are actually giving to each sector of your life. Then, compare that man circle to your imagined, and future life circle. If you had an ideal man circle what it look like?

Name the Elements and their magnitude
Work (or Purposeful activity income or not)
Family/ all relationships
Recreation (workouts and activity)
Avocations (not work, but part of who I am)
Rest/ sleep
RCP (reflection, contemplation, planning)
Faith/ belief/mediation/silence

SAMPLE LIFE CIRCLE

DRAW THE IDEAL ENRICHED MAN CIRCLE
Include the above elements or any that you desire. For the retired man, it may be three elements: Sail/ Rest/ Family, for another Volunteer/ Recreate/Rest. The permutations are endless. You can include your ideal activities, and experiment with what your life would be like living it. Some will see life without, active work, a dream,others are repulsed by the idea of retiring away from the workplace. What matters, here, is that this becomes your circle in the future.

The man circle is just another way to force becoming aware of how you are living your life, and how your time is actually being consumed. Manosophy requires an awareness of the present, and a sense of what the future may hold given certain life choices. The way time is spent or apportioned to the activities we have reviewed, actually defines who you are, and is not frivolous analysis. If you spend more time with your wife than you do anything else, but, work, is it time well spent?

AN IMPOSITION

This man circle and the way you use your time is critical to your self definition. The only thing we are losing, wasting, or using wisely is our time. So, how you spend it defines you.

Yet, there are elements that for a small expenditure of time can offer enormous benefits. They should be considered an essential to any ideal man circle. It is less than ten minutes a day to calm you, focus on your future, and clear your head whenever you need an instant retreat. We have offered these techniques earlier to handle anger, now put them into your daily circle.

THREE MINUTE MEDITATION- take the time to close your door, go into your car, or sit outside. And then, just clear your head, close your eyes, and let all thoughts go. Hold onto nothing. Breathe deeply, focus upon your breath, or a single image. Do this for three minutes, that's all. And return to another three if you need a head cleansing at any other part of the day. You can explore all meditation techniques, and apply them here, but this works!

THREE MINUTE REVIEW- take this three minutes at the end of the day. Focus upon that task you have targeted, either for professional advancement or soul work. Ask yourself, how are you doing against this goal. If it is speaking without cursing, ask yourself how did you do that day. Focus upon questions that are about issues or events you have promised to address. Make a mental note or write it into a journal. That's up to you, but just three minutes contemplating progress creates an awareness for your subconscious that you are on the way to changing behavior or expanding your horizons.

THE SIX DEEP BREATHS- this takes no time, a few seconds. But between activities or transitions, from office to car, car to meeting, before a phone call- take six very deep breaths. It will prepare you for the next event, oxygenate your brain, and calm your heart rate and blood pressure. The more important the next event, the more you need this. Do not judge it, or attach yourself to what is next, use the breaths to collect your thoughts, remind yourself of the outcome you want, and then move forward.

The Mind,Body, Spirit Circle

Just as the elements of activity define what we are doing day to day, less obvious,but, as critical to our well being is our balance of mind, body, and our spirit. They are ethereal, and lack being concrete, but, if they are not nurtured, the rest of our lives can crumble.

MIND

This is about mental state and the elasticity of your outlook. A well mind can focus on tasks, go easily from event to event, and not be obsessed with thoughts of the past, or current problems. The healthy mind retains perspective, some sense of humor, and always has a sense of proportion for the gravity,or not, of issues you confront most days.

You can be upset, fearful, and even, forgetful, but it does not define you. The range of common emotions are part of you, but do not overtake your actions. You hold to certain positions and opinions, but can listen, and respond to opposite viewpoints.

While you may be occasionally angry or combative, it is not your defining state. You can be moved emotionally, are not shutdown to your feelings, and can be empathetic. You may have periods,where you are confused, overwhelmed, and,even, depressed, but they usually fade overtime, and do not define your day to day actions.

The cultivation of this mind set, requires awareness of our mental states, and an understanding of what we must do to ease the stress we are under to allow the mind to release, relax, and recuperate from the pressure of any day or series of events.

BODY

The complexity of wellness for the body, is less obtuse, than the study of the mind. You know when you fell well, strong and fit. Men have an internal set point for how their body is functioning, based upon a set of feelings, the have established for themselves overtime. These markers are often not scientific, and anecdotal. A man may say he is well, if he can still play a half court, pick up game on weekends; run a mile in ten minutes; bench press his weight. Or, others have a mirror test, where they see an image that works for them, neither to heavy or light, or their eyes are clear, whatever.

Others, can obsess upon bio- markers that do offer a more scientific measure. Blood pressure; HDL; PSA tests;

weight/height ratios. These indicators do help measure wellness, but alone are as useless as a look in the mirror.

Your body wellness is a function of how you feel, your ability to do the tasks you want done; and is your body well enough for you to enjoy your life, and be epic. Compromising on body wellness, can destroy any life plan, and derail, even the most austere Manosophy.

SPIRIT

There is a source of power within you that drives you forward. It is untouchable, and in some ways unknowable, but, it is there in every man. Men with buoyant spirits are likely to stay with their plans, reach desired outcomes, and be happy in life. We all have our spirits drained, by hardship, loss and defeat. But, it is a bottomless pit of enthusiasm, if we cultivate its power.

For some this spirit is imbued with faith and a belief system that a higher power will always find a way, and our essence, this spirit, is linked to it. We need but to surrender to it, to release its power within us. For the less religious, the spirit is always there, and, as in other actions, we can through volition summon it to support all of our efforts.

It is this indomitable spirit that brings us back to what we must do; it is this spirit that forces us back up, after we have fallen; and it is this spirit that can allow us to believe that all of the grief, pain, and sacrifice, will end, and we will triumph.

Yet, the spirit can be drained. It to must be replenished with rest, solace, and new beginnings. You know when it is drained, and when it occupies the man circle with power.

The MBS Circle

This circle shows the energy of each aspect on your life at the time you draw it. If you are drained in spirit, it will hold less than a third of its power. And so with your mind and body.

The Perfect Circle- is different for each of us. Some feel strongest with more mind than body. Others function better with more body than mind energy. Chart your MBS now, then revisit, when you feel an energetic shift, around illness, excitement, and accomplishment. And, have a perfect circle drawn as well that is your goal to reach. Is it all three in balance, if not what works for you

Draw a Mind/Body/Spirit Circle

THE MAN CIRCLE OF A WORK HOUR

Of all the hours we pour into work, one hopes it is not only productive and purposeful, but also efficient. If we can get more done, and have time in each hour, for reflection, future thinking, and even, other activity it would revolutionize work. There are men who work at job that require their full attention for most of an hour. They know that what they are producing or manufacturing will not get completed on any other schedule. If you are a craftsmen, your perfect work hour is designed around the product and you know precisely what must be done to complete the job.

Not so, in our vastly expanding service and high technology economy. When you ask a man to circle out his work hour, the results are remarkably the same.

Actual work- 40 minutes
Phone Checking –work related – 10 minutes
Phone Checking- social- 5 minutes
Break, walking, socialization- 5 minutes
Sample Circle of work Hour

Of course, this is the perceived hour. When actually observed, you might expect, an average work hour is more like this:

Actual work – 20
Phone Checking- work related- 15
Phone Checking- social- 15
Phone calls work – 10
Break, walking, socialization-10-15

Considering the discrepancy, you can create an ideal work circle, that adapts to your productivity and creative needs. Again, there are no rules, except to provide the most powerful use of your skills over some period of time in the hour.

If you devote ten minutes, full bore, twice an hour, you will be many times more productive than most men at work. Then fill the other time, wisely, by thinking of the future, planning for work related breakthroughs, and future events. You would find it odd that most men, spend the least time on planning, idea generation, or preparation for future presentations. By focusing time on the work at hand in two ten minute, or any interval that is natural to your work, and then designate time for these other pursuits, your work, and the work of others will improve and foster more creative thinking.

IDEAL WORK HOUR GRAPH

The work
Phone
Social
Work
Planning/ ideas/ preparation

THE POWER OF THE CIRCLE

Devices that assist us in our thinking are not crutches to prop up weaknesses. The circles give us direct, obvious input on exactly what you are doing with your time. No Manosophy can have merit, if it only allows for imaginary concepts that suggest transformation and none occurs. Each time you draw a circle, it tells us you what you are doing, and show you how it differs from your ideal.

In fact, just the thinking about an ideal urges you towards its realization. When you draw it offers further encouragement. Certainly, a man can grow, establish a philosophy, and never draw a circle, jot down a note, keep a journal, or any record of activity. No one can pretend that there is one way to find your path to a better you. Still, these devices and tips may accelerate your momentum. After all, how far have you gotten making lists. Talking about change with your buddies, or failing to move forward because of the "forces" or your family and loved ones.

Everyone has an opinion. Most will tell you to stay put. Few give a good damn, if you do anything except earn, so they all can live off of your efforts. Nothing is the matter, with being a good man, who earns, supports, and loves those round him. But, it is not enough, if you are unhappy, unfulfilled, and want to reach for something more.

Nobody has to approve your quest. And they may laugh at you, and these circles, let them. The circles you draw is how you are living now, and can help you find another way.

And keep at, until as Elton says, "til we find our place, on the path unwinding"

WHAT ARE YOU PREPARED TO DO
Commit to drawing man circles
Life- now, next, ideal circle
Mind, Body, Spirit- now and ideal
The Work Hour Circle- now and ideal

CHAPTER XI

The Warrior Within

"Given enough time, any man can master the physical. With enough knowledge, any man may become wise. It is the true warrior who can master both.. and surpass the result."

Tien T'ai

Inside each of us, is a warrior spirit. It is the essence of all men that when challenged,we can battle for what is right and to sustain our way of life. We cannot know if can summon the courage of men in actual battle, who in an instant summon their extraordinary will to save lives, imperil themselves and act with courage. Yet, our daily efforts require the same devotion, and a life long commitment to act upon values that embody this warrior spirit.

Warriors are well trained, have an awareness of their powers, understand their weaknesses, and act with proportional response based upon the level of threat. They also are not tentative when they strike, nor distracted until a threat or challenge is met with a fearless response. The ability to act with discipline is the mark of a man who has honed his physical skills while understanding when and how to approach challenges.

The traits that define a modern warrior are not out of reach, and can be blended into any manosophy. It begins with finding a path to earn income, provide for yourself and others, and do it with enough resilience to build a meaningful life. The rigors of accomplishing that might seem enough, but, it becomes manifest through "right action". The very application of these traits accelerates the warrior towards significant life goals.

Warrior Traits

Honesty- knowing what you can handle, your strengths and weaknesses. Taking an inventory of your skills to accomplish results, and planning to acquire new skills, when needed, before you take action on a project or engage in a new venture.

Backbone – understanding when you must act, and standing by your choices. Acting upon your decisions and instincts, and yielding only when evidence indicates your initial actions need to be amended. Deciding, what you can give up and what you cannot.

Adaptable- realizing that some lines of attack may be closed or are ineffective. Pursuing a path with vigor, and then, changing techniques or approaches to stay on the game plan. This is calling an audible before or during a course of action.

Kindness- it is a powerful weapon to achieve outcomes. When the instinct may be to offer harsh response, or allow the indulgence of acting coarsely, it rarely pays the dividend of treating people warmly, and with empathy.

Resilient- no matter how many knock downs, a warrior is always rising. It is this quality that can provide wins and results, even, in the face of obvious defeat. No person, problem, relationship exists in stasis. As you continue to act, the obstacles energy can shift and offer an opening.

No Excuses- there are always obstacles and reasons to stop action. Some are valid and must be heeded. But, often, the excuse is a crutch that releases a man from continuing to fight for objectives. It is an exit strategy that is not honest, and avoids the facing of flaws that once realized can be overcome.

Low Drama- there is a tendency to create high levels of emotion, surrounding life events. All relationships, and exchanges of personalities ignite some level of emotion and drama into our lives. The difficulty arises if it becomes out of proportion with the intensity of the exchange. Living, as though, any of these moments, even divorce, loss, or high romance should have an overwhelming presence can damage your progress and game plan.

Awareness- having a focus on the matter at hand, not being distracted by other arguments, people or concerns. Linking one intense moment to another and creating an understanding of how they form a chain of events. This awareness is both of the current situation and how it links to a larger frame of reference. You are not narrow minded and prepared to learn about other matters, ideas, and concepts.

Patience- not everything can happen on a forced

timeline. Success may come past an imposed deadline, or before it. Knowing, and allowing, for events to find their own pace may require less obvious effort, and conserve effort.

Ultimately, the warrior spirit emerges when you cultivate it, and use it each day to guide your actions. The practice is using these traits to solve problems and achieve outcomes you have targeted to progress in your transformation. The challenge is to act with them, and create a discipline to use these traits, as they are valuable tools to accomplish objectives. They do not exist alone in your make up. There is a power within, that is variously defined as Qi or Chi, or hara. It resides throughout your body, running like an electrical charge, pulsating throughout your nervous system.

Modern men often deny its presence. Yet, when you must act with great power, or out of total fatigue, it can be observed. A boxer gets up off the mat and delivers a knockout punch, a quarterback manages a hail Mary, a man lifts a car off a child. And you, find the power to get through a brutal day of work, or end a bad relationship. Everything difficult can be assisted by this power within, an inner energy.

The mystics from India, meditation gurus, and even Tibetan Zen monks all claim we can access this power through being silent, clearing our minds through meditation, and living a life on some purpose. To the believers in a mythical, ancient, Kingdom called Shambhala, like Shangri La, it is called, "riding the windhorse", or getting your energy marshaled to float or ride above problems and life concerns. You may not seek it, or decide to meditate to reveal it, but, to most observers, regardless of what you call it, there does seems to be an inner force, that can offer us, a special reserve when most needed. If as a warrior you are open to new ideas and are expanding horizons, going in search of your Qi has merit.

"Only one who devotes himself to a cause with his whole body and soul can be a true master. For this reason, mastery demands, all of a person" Deng Ming-Dao

It may seem obvious that the other side of warrior traits are actions, and habits that hold us back from our goals. Honesty requires that we face what actions we exhibit that are, perhaps, keeping us from changing our persona. These qualities take us backward in our progression, are difficult to face and expunge. They are obvious to others, and less so to ourselves. But, the admission that they exist, frees us to eradicate them from our self definition. The challenge is to identify what might be hampering our game plan, and, have the warrior's courage to face them and overcome their hold upon us.

Comportment- is an old fashioned concept that embodies the totality of outward appearance. The mothering influences while seemingly a pain to consider, do matter. A man who never cares about his posture, and sulks round shouldered is seen in a different light than a man who stands and sits tall. Putting things in their place, keeping a clean workplace, and being tidy is a simple declaration of order. Dressing in wrinkled and unmatched clothes, never appearing pressed or thoughtfully put together can impact perception, and, diminish your perception of yourself. This is about owning your presence and what you want to project to the world to fit your philosophy. It maybe that slumped, and unkempt is your mantra. So be it. But do it with flair, thoughtfulness, and an understanding of whether your look and posture meets your own life standard.

Narcissist- there is some element of this in all men. This worship of the self, to the exclusion of the value of others in our lives. Taken to extremes this view can destroy even the most worthy goals, as every action is filtered through the ego. Without question the drive to be this insular success story can generate great men, careers, and results. But, for most of us, it can limit our lives, close us off from relationships, and narrow the experience of life.

Misogyny- this distain for women, or refusal to see them as equal players, is a flaw that holds men back from a balanced game plan. It is natural to see women as adversaries in the workplace, as obstacles to freedom, or as grand manipulators. But, when feelings about an individual infect your view of all women, then, you are projecting a level of disrespect that can, not only, stymie your plans, but damage your outlook for all time.

Foul Mouth- nothing more clearly targets a man, than his language. If you are around men who use expletives in every sentence, you establish a view of them that is not salutary. Even in locker rooms and fields of play, a regular pattern of modifiers that are f..ing this and f..ing that, say more about them, than they expect. Everyone curses out of dismay and, at times, for emphasis. But, cleaning up your language, even when angry, speaks to a man under control and thoughtful about his impact on those around him.

Drinking to Excess- this is common for men who socialize with alcohol as an element of relaxation. The number of men, who drink to excess on weekends, at ballparks, or any other male gathering is millions each week. Often men, will claim they are under control, and most are to some extent. Yet, being seen as a man who is often "plastered" when he is not working, is more than unattractive. While, you are binging, what of your game plan is getting done, and are you fulfilling your personal operating philosophy goals?

Indecisive- the failure to decide upon an action and then proceed, is another negative trait. Often, when faced with the need to take steps to achieve an outcome, there will be hesitation and, even, fear. The path to confidence is action, in a forceful and non tentative display of momentum. The trick here is to do something. The mere act of a decision, emboldens more action.

Two Faced- saying one thing and doing another, or, promising a result and failing to deliver. Men may also say one thing to one person, and on the same issue, say something else to another to avoid conflict, please them, or con someone. This action, is always revealed, and results in a loss of trust. It also shows an essential flaw of having no backbone. Eventually, the tactic defines the man, and he is abandoned by more honest associates.

Non Stop Talk- an irritating, if not confounding flaw. These men are so engaged in their own narrative that they create a barrage of sentences and viewpoints that overwhelm others in a conversation. Often the rapidity of the narrative is a defense against having to actually take action, or, internalize the debate. Eliminating this, and slowing down the rate of verbal engagement can quickly change perceptions of your value to problem solving, and, enhance other social interactions.

Addiction- regardless of the substance, alcohol, drugs, or opiates, men can function with addictions and are often able to succeed at achieving goals, for some time. But, the trajectory of all men who are addicted is the same. There is a fall, and it be fatal. There is nothing manly, cool, or useful in being an addict. Every mans' goal is to help others seek treatment, intervene where needed, and free other men from the grip of substance abuse.

Not Merely Men

We are not just here to get up, earn, procreate, and expire. There is more to each of us. A mixture of qualities, traits and instincts that drive us towards superior lives. The challenge is to unravel the better instincts, ignite the good traits, and overcome conditioning that is holding us back from our destiny.

Katsumoto: You believe a man can change his destiny?

Nathan Algren: I think a man does what he can until his destiny is revealed to him

The Last Samurai

What a man does as he waits defines him. Your Manosophy is precisely that guide to a game plan for your life. Algren sees the world as a battlefield, and the hard life requires a Western soldiers code. To the Last Samurai, Katsumoto, there is a sense that the path of a man is pre-determined, and the code, Bushido, when followed allows for dignity along that path, where one can be poet and warrior.

It is for each man to choose his path, and the traits

needed along the way to complete the very unique and personal journey. There are foundational elements as expressed here that advance or retard that forward progress. Still, it must be your game plan, your choice of which code you will follow.

The ability you have within you to decide what you embellish, work on,or reject is entirely within your grasp. The challenge is to do any of it because you will it to be so, based upon a trajectory you see for yourself, not one dictated by a lover, wife, mother or boss. This is where the warrior within emerges and can be marshaled to assist in your own heroic journey. All of this may sound mythical or distant from your story, but, it is not at all. You have a mission to find the best man you can become, and you will fight against forces, some you can control and others you cannot.

And, there is victory lurking in these battles, for all men. Certainly, they will not be each day or moment, but, over time being consistently committed to your destiny revealing itself will offer a path of value and enjoyment. Warriors are not men of remorse or sadness, they are about commitment, a value directed life, and a self worth that comes from purposeful actions.

There is nothing stopping you from being that person by releasing the warrior within you.

WHAT ARE YOU PREPARED TO DO

List your warrior traits?
What traits can you enhance day to day?
Assess any negative influences?

Set up a plan with milestones to eradicate bad traits, in one month.

Imagine a perfect man circle, a perfect mind/ body/ spirit circle, then, ask yourself why you cannot achieve that, and then go after it for one week.

CHAPTER XII

Happiness Is Your Birthright

"Follow Your Bliss "

Joseph Campbell

For most men the pursuit of happiness is an episodic quest. Happiness comes and goes and is not the single minded pursuit suggested by Thomas Jefferson, a man of the Enlightenment, nor by, mythologist, Joseph Campbell. Which is not to say that men are not happy, at times, or satisfied at times in their lives. Yet, men are usually more engaged in making things work for others, and guaranteeing their happiness than their own. While the question of happiness is often asked of others, it is rarely put to the man following his path. "Are you happy?" is the most infrequently asked question of a modern man in a free society.

The result is that it is often not on a man's top ten list of things to accomplish. It is seen more as a bonus of a life well lived, than the direction or goal of that life. So if man has a moment of bliss, it is often either a fleeting emotion, or the result of his accomplishment, or vicariously of his team, or family member. The essential purity and all encompassing joy that comes from a life directed at happiness resides in few lives. Thus,when men are asked to rate their happiness it is often situational, and not embedded in a personal operating philosophy.

When you ask yourself to rate your happiness, do it across two different continuums. The first is in a emotional context. Are you happy, right now, emotionally? Do you feel more lightness than dark, and feel good about things?

Emotional Happiness

Dark/   Unhappy..
Generally Happy

Then, rate yourself on happiness as defined by overall quality of life and achievement.

Good Life...Lousy

Somewhere along both of these lines your happiness quotient rests. As you would expect, most men fall between the polarities. The ideal state is obviously, not in some hallucination of euphoria, but somewhere more modest. The emotional scale can score higher,since any single event can bring immediate emotional highs. A win in any pursuit can yield enormous happiness and a high. Just ask a man who finally gets that promotion, a date with his most adored gal, or scores in anything.

The Manosophy goal is to construct a game plan that encourages happiness, and views it as a regular and reachable benefit over the long term. It has been a part of philosophical thought far before the Enlightenment and our founders inclusion of it as an unalienable right given by God to all men. Our old friend Aristotle saw it as a centerpiece of mans' driving force, in his treatise on ethics in 350 BCE. To him it was, in Greek, Eudaimonia, or a will to be happy. For him a man was happy who acted rationally, was a thinker, and realized everyone wanted the same shot at being happy.

In his study of religions and myths, Joseph Campbell found that all heroes, in the tales of heroic journeys, fought the forces, to achieve "bliss", which led him to proselytize,

"I say, follow your bliss and don't be afraid, and the doors will open where you didn't know they were going to be. If you follow your bliss, doors will open for you that wouldn't have opened for anyone else."

All faiths from Buddhism to the Abrahamic traditions, have a place for happiness. The very pursuit of it, not a sin or indiscretion, but a positive, even a "good deed". Of course, that faith based happiness comes with adherence to codes, rules, and guidelines, not, rules you establish on your own. Even, St. Thomas Aquinas, "the last end.. which is happiness", as the epitaph for righteous men. Yet, even with all of this seeming support, how much time are modern men devoting to their happiness?

There are some psychologists who contend that America would improve in all aspects,if we charted and devoted a cabinet seat to wellness and happiness. In Bhutan, a tiny, mountainous, monarchy, they actually assess the Gross Happiness Product, a GHP, to monitor the mood of the state. That seems far a field for our country, but as an individual it just might help in making happiness a priority in your game plan. Why not have happiness as a requirement of your life, rather than as a lucky bonus. If we begin to pay attention to our happiness and act as if we are happy, it may suddenly appear in our lives and enhance our other goals and pursuits. The team or athlete that plays happy, and with optimism, is more likely to have more energy, less fatigue, and actually enjoy the game of life.

There is a zone, when you enter it, happiness ensues. You are making love and there is no other world, but the two of you; you are playing the best round of golf ever; your business presentation seems to go by in a minute; that cabinet you are making is happening without effort. These are in the zone experiences, happiness explodes inside of you because it is fueling emotions and a sense of grand accomplishment. The mastery of this duality is what happens as we are "in the flow".

One, Mihaly Csikszentmihalyi has offered this theory of "flow" and the power of this state to accomplish tasks, and direct a game plan. In his, "Flow: The Psychology of Optimal Experience", this Hungarian psychologist describes happiness, as most likely to occur, when a man is in this state of absorption. As one of the father's of positive psychology, Mihaly indicates that creating a life with enough episodes of this flow, would likely assist in offering a journey that is more about happiness than not.

Neither Csikszentmihalyi, nor Campbell expect that this quest for flow or bliss is a constant daily event, but, that its very presence with regularity can bring both meaning and energy that overcomes the days' fatigue. Activity that breeds absorption and/or meaning seems to be an ingredient of happiness for men. While, it seems assuredly to offer the upbeat and optimistic world view, why is it so few men seek it out, and plan it into their daily activity.

It is largely, the result of procrastination and compartmentalization. Joy and happiness are relegated to optional pursuits that will be pursued either when the serious work of the day is concluded or on a vacation. This delaying tactic, can go on for decades, and what a man wants to do is eclipsed by what he must do. Even work on purpose, while gratifying may not offer the ingredient of absorption and unbounded positive emotional feedback available in the zone. So, even though it is a source of pleasure, and,even, accomplishment, it is still relegated to a second class status.

Martin Seligman, a noted past President of the American Psychological Association, and an iconic purveyor of the theory of positive psychology believes that most men can be happy. To "Marty" happiness is a composite of what he calls PERMA. Positive emotion, Engagement, Relationships, Meaning, and Achievement. His view parallels other experts, who see the confluence of positive experiences, emotions, and achieving goals as steps to some degree of happiness. Still, being happy is a volitional accomplishment. While, a man may be in circumstances that just happen to make him happy by good fortune or serendipity, for most men guiding activity and selecting circumstances is more likely to result in general happiness.

What makes you Happy?

If you could put aside the daily activities, the burdens of making a living, building a family or career, what would make you happy right now? Can you create a list of just twelve things that would? There need be no time frame or limits. What does a happy list look like.

Here is a sample,
Happy List
A warm dinner of eggplant parmesan
Trek to Everest basecamp
Spend an evening just making love
Taking the kids to a Superbowl
Doing an epic journey- row the Pacific ocean
Learn Spanish
Take parents to Hawaii for anniversary
Get a nap on Saturday afternoons
Volunteer for delivering meals to seniors
Help young men plan their lives
Drink Irish coffee at Buena Vista in San Francisco
Get raises for staff

Make your List of Twelve (it may take more time than you think, take your time)

1.
2.
3.
4.
5.
6.
7.
8.
9.
10.
11.
12.

It was probably, not as easy to accomplish, as you might have thought. And, you know why. Men are just not oriented towards such pursuits. We may plan, many other things, but our own happiness is not usually on the list. This exercise tests our meddle to force ourselves to find activities and plan for circumstances that bring us closer to the flow, the zone, and our bliss.

This penchant to delay bliss, and joy always catches a man, when crisis comes upon him. Ask the man who has stage four cancer, or lived a long life and still has many regrets. These regrets are often about things undone, and happiness deferred. There is nothing negative about bucket lists to encourage and prompt our imaginations. If we can imagine it, it can become manifest. At least, writing down the possibilities begins a biological and psychic shift that may bring it about. None of this is linear.

Happiness does not just arrive, it requires planning, thought, and action to achieve. But, as a man you must want this unalienable right. You have the right to pursue in a free society, it is tragic to waste the opportunity.

Tim McGraw sings it best in his classic," Live Like You Were Dying"

"Someday I hope you get the chance, to live like you were dying. Like tomorrow was a gift and you've got eternity to think about, what you'd do with it what could you do with it? What did you do with it? What would you do with it?"

Are you living like you were dying?

WHAT ARE YOU PREPARED TO DO?

Create a list of what you want to do that will bring you happiness

A list of emotional items (love making to sky diving)
A list of accomplishments
What activities put you in the zone?
When you flow what are you doing?

CHAPTER XIII

The World Changes When You Do

'You must be the change you wish to see in the world '

Mahatma Gandhi

As you watch a stadium fill with fans, mostly men, or scan your local gym, note that most of these guys have no game plan for their lives. If you pull one side and just ask what is their philosophy of life, you may get a sentence or two or one of the standard phrases. But, for most men, life is just lived, with some tenuous plan, to find a job, pay bills, get married, have kids, and sprinkle in some favorite pursuits, and die. What they could become, develop into, or rise to, is often left to the "forces", destiny, or God. And, whatever happiness comes into their life is as much by chance as design.

Manosophy provides a different path where a man actually considers using his freedoms to transform himself into the best man he can become. This transformation is not magic, nor inaccessible to any man of any age. It requires a determination to chart a game plan that allows for growth of personality, intellect and a degree of emotional control. This allows a man to create his own personal operating philosophy that gives him a foundation of beliefs and actions that incrementally drive a change of outlook.

Without a game plan, you are more likely to respond to stimuli and make choices that seem appropriate for the moment, or offer a way for the short term. No coach goes into any contest, let alone a championship, without a game plan. Your life is the ultimate contest, and without a plan and operating philosophy, you will find your plays limited, and worse, the plays themselves, may be the plays of someone else. You want to throw long, do razzle dazzle, play without abandon, but you can only run for short yardage.

So many men capitulate to others, out of love, fear, and weariness. The rigors of doing well at work, growing a career, paying debts, and being an attentive husband or boyfriend, and a devoted son, can seem overwhelming. There is little time for rest in a crowded schedule, let alone life planning. Yet, without any plan, the game you are playing, this life of yours, is adrift. And, when you finally decide to direct it, there will be powerful forces that will deter your actions. So, most men grow as they can, retreat to the rutted life, only to emerge again. This tentative process requires more energy, and is more prone to failure than a true philosophy that fosters a game plan.

Now there are no guarantees that planning, and thinking about who you are and who you want to be has a lock on success. You may do all that is presented here; decide on an operating philosophy; adopt an outlook; review choices based on outcomes; face your fears; advance your best traits; and, still be rocked by life. But life is going to come and get you anyway, plan or not. The best chance you have to evolve and become the man you want to become, is by having some plan or roadmap of your dreams, and then when detours come, at least you know where the hell you are.

There is calm that befits a man with a philosophy of his life. A steadiness in purpose and design. He understands that there are manipulators out to strangle his spirit, forces, he cannot control, and barriers he cannot see, until he is upon them. But, a game plan based upon a personal operating philosophy has the quality of slowing down the ball, and allowing a man to see the seams, before a swing. As the challenges slow, there is time for better decisions and actions. A chance for some thought, the marshaling of inner strength, and the certainty of a precise strike at a target.

The decision to begin this journey has started with this handbook on Manosophy. You may have found it amusing, helpful in some regard, or even, feel compelled to begin the change within you. But, that you started it, shows that inside you there is a yearning to be better, to find something more for yourself. This philosophy thing is internal, and some might say, selfish. And, it is. Transforming who you are is about that face in your mirror. It takes considerable will and courage to admit that there can be something else, that there is an uncharted path for you, a path that will offer purpose, and, even, happiness. Others will offer disdain, claim it is unworthy, or unmanly. They are afraid of what you will become, frightened of the power of change; for, they fear you leave them behind. And you may. Yet, it is just as likely that they will be with you and empowered by a more resolute, and content partner in life.

A CHECKLIST FOR MANOSOPHY

Review these milestones, and begin to construct your game plan:

What is your personal operating philosophy?
What are your goals, outcomes, dreams
What is your outlook ?
Optimism and its limits
Can you list the traits you bring to your philosophy
Are you prepared to battle the Four Horsemen
Shame, Approval, Guilt and Fear
Living a more active, strenuous life
Decide what you do believe and examine your faith
Deal with Sex and Respect for women
Use outcome analysis to make decisions
Employ Man Circles and Thought maps as tools
Cultivate the Warrior Spirit
Allow happiness into your life

ESSENTIAL INQUIRY

You can begin anywhere, after you decide to declare this is the life I want; this is how I will live it; and, this is what I will become. The answer to these inquires of yourself may not last, but, it provides a starting point for change. You may decide that all of this was just an exercise in thinking about a mans' life and no action is required. That is your choice.

You can have a successful, and happy life with no

planning, no outlook, and no stated philosophy. Yet, what could your life have been? What might you have achieved? These questions remain unanswered, until, the epiphany of disease befalls you; a loss derails you; or, at the end of it all, the regrets outweigh the accomplishments.

Let us conclude with the words of Charles Bukowski, street poet, former drunk, gambler, and everyman:

"If you're going to try go all the way. Otherwise, don't even start. This could mean losing girlfriends, wives, relatives, and maybe even your mind. ..If you're going to try, go all the way. There is no other feeling like that. You will be alone with the Gods, and the night will flame with fire. You will ride life straight to perfect laughter. It's the only good fight there is."

Bukowski, Factotum

It is your life, decide.

We Are Not Them

December 2017

As I write this ending, men are once again being stereotyped by main stream media and a new phalanx of proto-feminists. This attempt is to lump all men into a subset of men who engage in sexual misconduct, and have harassed, or criminally attacked women. We are not these men. Most men, and all who want to create a personal operating philosophy to guide their lives, respect women and have clarity on the boundaries of sexual engagement.

To be clear sexual misconduct exists, and runs a gamut of abuses. These include unwanted flirting, creating a "hostile" work environment, and, can escalate to predatory assault and rape. All are odious to any man who hopes to transform himself into a better person. But, these behaviors are not ingrained, in all men. They are examples of aberrant acts that come from a complex of personality disorders. To ascribe this behavior to all men is a travesty.

For historical reference, for readers in later years, here are the culprits, and the charges and admissions. It began with movie mogul and Miramax studio head, Harvey Weinstein, who after years of abusive behavior had 83 women come forward. Some claimed he coaxed them into sex, while he stood dressed only with a robe, and his penis on display. He was fired, lost his awards, and standing in Hollywood. Still, he is staging a comeback to fight some of the charges.

Two media anchors, highly regarded also were fired for sexual misconduct. Matt Lauer of the Today Show, served as its host from 1997- 2017. He coaxed women into his office, offered his penis to them, allegedly raped one, and offered sex toys to another. And, Charlie Rose, anchor of CBS's morning news and PBS, interview program, a 75 year old, intellect, emerged naked before interns and assistants, and attempted to intimidate women for decades into his bed. Both were summarily fired.

But, it does not end there. In politics, a Judge Roy Moore, running for U.S. Senate in Alabama was accused of attempting to have sex with younger women, charges he denied. But, Minnesota Senator, Al Franken admitted forcing himself on women, even forcing his tongue into the mouth of a former model. He also admitted to being "warm" to women on campaign outings, including grabbing their butts or hugging their breasts.

This failure to understand or just avoid boundaries extended to men who prefer other men as well. The issue is the same, regardless of sexual preference. Power, control, and influence over others gives the abuser a belief, they are above the law, and, in fact, entitled to the encounter. They do not see it as a violation, but, a reward for their achievements. Often the abuser will diminish the victims claims, saying it was "just" a meeting, a kiss, or a one- time event. They refuse to admit guilt, and offer up public relations apologies, but, what they are admitting is that they were caught, and no one understands them. Most have a deep seeded and long held poor self esteem, they act out like pre-pubescent boys, afraid of the loss of love or its denial.

Kevin Spacey was an actor of justifiable acclaim. Yet, he was unable to stem his addiction to chasing young men. His vaunted theater groups, his position of esteem, where not enough to curtail his penchant for touching young men, and encouraging sexual acts. And, even for master conductor, James Levine, from the New York, Metropolitan Opera, he was struck by allegations, he bedded a young man for years, and took him naked to his bed from performance to performance. And the boy claims he was one of many.

Each has its own psychological reason, a complex of upbringing, genetic proclivities, and the belief that being accomplished removes the boundaries of civility and law. These men are pariahs to other men, their good work does not mitigate their treatment of others. The tendency to define the whole by its aberrant parts is natural for mass media, and for feminists out to define men by their standards. The fight for all men is to define ourselves, get on our own paths, and construct lives of purpose, founded on respect for women, and a morality that is not situational, but, sacrosanct.

When we gaze at how men are doing, there are other examples of men acting without thought about the consequences of their actions. Fraternal organizations are under fire for hazing rituals, encouraging binge drinking, and treating women as objects. The role models have faded, as men embrace alternate cultures from hip- hop, and its misogyny, to video games and their altered reality. Still, there is great hope for the evolution and development of men in a free society.

The core values are there; the drive to succeed; the devotion to a better future remains part of all of us. What remains is to not let the definition others have of men to stop our own progression. We are not them, and what we are to become is up to us, where our spirit takes us is a far better place than the critics can ever imagine.

The stories of Weinstein, Franken, Rose, Lauer, Spacey and the rest will eventually fade away, as like a phase of the moon. And, your story will begin a new phase that will end with a brightness for men who have found a guiding spirit within them that will make us all the better.

"POPS" 2017

Printed in the United States
By Bookmasters